Experiencing

CHRIST JESUS

The Redeemer

Perez Publishing

Breaking through... Breaking out

Experiencing

CHRIST JESUS

The Redeemer

JAMES EKOR-TAH

Unless otherwise indicated, all Scripture quotations are taken from the New King James Version of the Bible. Copyright © 1979, 1980, 1982, by Thomas Nelson, Inc. Used by permission. All rights reserved.

Scripture quotations marked NIV are taken from the Holy Bible: New International Version ® NIV ®. Copyright © 1973, 1978, 1984 by International Bible Society. Used by permission of Zondervan Publishing House. All rights reserved.

Experiencing Christ Jesus, The Redeemer

ISBN: 978-1-945055-16-4

Printed in the United States of America
Published by Perez Publishing

Copyright © 2019 James Ekor-Tah

2029 Burnside Dr.
Frederick MD 21702
info@woflt.com | www.woflt.com

All rights reserved. No portion of this publication may be reproduced, stored in a retrieval system, or transmitted in any form or by any means – for example, electronic, photocopy, recording – without the prior written permission of the publisher. The only exception is brief quotations in printed reviews.

The author has emphasized some words in Scripture quotations in italicized type.

Cover design: Jean Fabrice, solacevibe@gmail.com

DEDICATION

To my beloved wife and confidant, Julienne Abigail, a faithful partner in the high calling of God upon my life.

To my beloved children: Elizabeth Grace, Madeleine Shekinah, Jamie Rhema; to Kathy Hicks, and to all who love God, to those who are the called according to His purpose.

TABLE OF CONTENT

Acknowledgements --- 9
Forward -- 11
Introduction --- 19

Chapter 1: Jesus Christ the Same Yesterday,
           Today and Forever------------------------------ 27
Chapter 2: Who is Jesus Christ? --------------------------- 31
Chapter 3: The Power in The Name of Jesus ------------- 39
Chapter 4: The Ongoing Ministry of Jesus----------------- 54
Chapter 5: Redemption in Christ---------------------------- 69
Chapter 6: The Redemption Work of Christ -------------- 87
Chapter 7: Reconciliation in Christ. ----------------------- 103
Chapter 8: Identity in Christ ------------------------------ 113
Chapter 9: The Authority of The Believer --------------- 125
Chapter 10: Experiencing Redemption ------------------ 137
Appendix A: You Can Receive Christ Today ------------ 147
Appendix B: Declare Who You Are in Christ. --------- 149

Acknowledgments

All the glory goes to my Precious Savior, The Lord Jesus, who is forever blessed and highly lifted; far above all names and thrones, for there is none like Him. I thank You, Lord, for Your manifold grace which enabled me to complete this work. For without You, our existence on earth has no meaning.

I thank my wife Julienne Abigail who is my faithful partner in life and the ministry entrusted to us. Sweetheart, thank you for being my audience of one. This book is a result of your constant reminders and encouragement to put into writing the many little messages that we shared during our family devotions.

I want to express a special thank you to the Lord for "Daddy" David Atogho, of blessed memory, for the father figure that he was to me and to so many. He took the time to read through the manuscript of this book, and corrected its grammar and offered many valuable suggestions, which I

Acknowledgements

gladly accepted and are included in this book. I consider his work and input into this book as valuable as that of an editor.

I will always remain grateful to Professor Joeseph Mbafor and His beloved wife who are dear parents of ours, (me and my family). Thanks a lot for your many prayers and parental care both practically and in ministry.

I want to say a special thank you to the members of my local congregation of Word of Life Tabernacle, Frederick, for your prayers and support. Thanks for the confidence that you all have towards me. It is a privilege to serve as your pastor.

I want to especially thank my uncle, Mr. George Keboa, and his dear wife Mrs. Augusta Keboa who took care of me and provided for my every need during my formative years. In the same breath, I say thanks to my aunt Mrs. Cecilia Enow for being the mother that you are. I am eternally grateful to God for your sacrificial investments of love and care which laid the foundation that gave me a sense of self-worth.

I am grateful to the Lord for my mother, Mrs. Elizabeth Esong, of blessed memory. A mother who believed in me and told me that I was special. A strong mother who was selfless in her love for all her children.

Forward

Christian Faith's experience and practice are the fruit of Revelation by the Lord God. When Jesus asked His disciples who they thought He was, only Peter gave the right answer: "You are the Christ, the Son of the Living God." Jesus told him: "You are blessed, for this was not revealed to you by man, but by My Father in Heaven."

Bearing this in mind, thus several questions arise. After spending three years with Jesus, did the disciples know, understand and experience salvation, redemption, reconciliation with God, and the power of the Holy Spirit – before the Day of Pentecost? They did not even understand the why and wherefore of the crucifixion and the resurrection, even though Jesus told them several times that he would be arrested, tried and tortured, crucified unto death, and that He would rise the third day. They faced the shocking, and awesome events of His trial and suffering, crucifixion, resurrection and ascension step after step, till the outpouring

Forward

of the Holy Spirit at the Pentecost. Then, they now began to experience Christ Jesus, the Redeemer.

The Church is full of people who know the story of the birth, life, death, and resurrection of Jesus Christ very well, but who know nothing of the saving, sanctifying, justifying and liberating power of the Ministry of His Word, crucifixion, resurrection, ascension, and glorification. I confess that it was not until after 30 years in the Church that, the Lord opened my inner eyes and I understood why I continued to fall, sin and suffer oppressions, despite "being a Christian." It was when I was reading Watchman Nee's book, "The Normal Christian Life" on the 23rd of September, 1976, that the scales fell from my eyes, and I understood the gracious and blessed victory Jesus Christ gave me, (and to all else who believe and receive Him, along with a revelation of the New Birth), when I was crucified with Him, died in Him, was buried with Him, and raised with Him by the Holy Spirit, that I received the New Life – in Jesus! I wept and cried with a mixture of anguish and joy why I had never read and understood Romans 6:1-14 those many years.

Pastor James Ekor-Tah braves the subject of a Victorious Christian Life by pressing the case for a daily pursuit of God's purpose in sending His Beloved Son to come and redeem us, restore us to Himself. We can happily enjoy

Experiencing Christ Jesus, The Redeemer

His holy, righteous, healthy, wealthy, triumphant and glorious life.

A common saying runs thus: "Practice makes perfect!" Throughout the Bible, God's sworn and faithful word, we and all disciples are taught:

> ➤ "Be strong and very courageous, be careful to obey all the law My servant Moses gave you... Do not let this Book of the Law depart from your mouth; meditate on it day and night so that you may be careful to do everything written on it. Then you will be PROSPEROUS AND SUCCESSFUL. Have I not commanded you?" (Joshua 1:7-9)
>
> ➤ "All authority in heaven and on earth has been given to Me. Therefore, go and make disciples of all nations, baptizing them in the name of the Father, and of the Son and of the Holy Spirit, and teaching them to obey everything I have commanded you. And surely, I will be with you always, to the very end of the age." (Matthew 28:18-20)
>
> ➤ Jesus replied: "I saw Satan fall like lightning from heaven. I have given you authority to trample on snakes and scorpions and to overcome all the power of the enemy; nothing will harm you. However, do not rejoice that the spirits submit to

Forward

you, but rejoice that your names are written in heaven." (Luke 10:18-20)

- "I tell you the truth, anyone who has faith in me will do what I have been doing, he will do even greater things than these because I am going to the Father. And I will do whatever you ask in my name, so that the Son may bring glory to the Father. You may ask me for anything in my name, and I will do it." (John 14:12-14)

- "I am the vine; you are the branches. If a man remains in Me and I in him, he will bear much fruit; apart from Me you can do nothing." (John 15:5)

- "If we have been united with Him in His death, we will certainly also be united with Him in His resurrection. For we know that our old self was crucified with Him so that the body of sin might be rendered powerless, that we should no longer be slaves to sin – because anyone who has died has been freed from sin." (Romans 6:5-7)

- "Therefore, if anyone is in Christ, he is a new creation: the old has gone, the new has come. All this is from God who has reconciled us to Himself through Christ and gave us the ministry of reconciliation… God made Him who had no sin to be sin for us so that in Him we might become the righteousness of God." (2 Corinthians 5:17-21)

- "I have been crucified with Christ and I no longer live but Christ lives in me. The life I live in the body, I live by faith in the Son of God, who loves me and gave Himself for me." (Galatians 2:20)

- "I keep asking that the God of our Lord Jesus Christ, the glorious Father, may give you the Spirit of wisdom and revelation, so that you may know Him better. I pray also that the eyes of your heart may be enlightened in order that you may know the hope to which He has called you, the riches of His glorious inheritance in the saints, and His incomparable power for us who believe. That power is like the working of His mighty strength which he exerted in Christ when He raised Him from the dead and seated Him at the right hand in the heavenly realms..." (Ephesians 1:17-23)

- "And God raised us up with Christ and seated us with Him in the heavenly realms in Christ Jesus, in order that in the coming age, He might show the incomparable riches of His grace, expressed in His kindness to us in Christ Jesus." (Ephesians 2:6,7)

Pastor Ekor-Tah concludes his study with Biblical declarations of who we are and what we have in Christ and exhorts all serious believers to daily declare them (over and in themselves), in full assurance of faith that transforms profoundly.

What is challenging about this book is that, as the conscious reader of the Bible reads the book, his inner eyes are the more opened to appreciate not only the great price the Lord God paid to redeem, ransom and repossess us from sin and its consequences but a greater understanding and desire to internalize more revelations of what Jesus Christ is currently doing to ensure our daily experience of the reality of having made us partakers of God's own very nature. Believing is acting on the Word; and as Jesus lives to intercede for us, the Holy Spirit will do more and more in us through the Word.

Whereas redemption is legal and has been accomplished (it is a finished work! We are complete in Him). The New Birth is vital – it is now, and we must act our faith now and each day, as the Lord abides in us and us in Him, triumphing in faith, not by sight, feeling or hearing. Experiencing redemption in Christ is having absolute dominion over Satan, sin and demonic oppression. It is enjoying the peace that flows from a clear conscience before God and praising and worshiping the God who meets all my needs infinitely.

He that is in Me (Father, Son, Holy Spirit) is greater than he who is in the world – so in Christ, I am more than a conqueror!

David Atogho, *Elder (1936-2017)*
Christian Missionary Fellowship International & Associated Churches
August 2014, Yaoundé, Cameroon.

INTRODUCTION

For those of us who know God as Father God, our God is in the business of redemption - the redemption of Mankind. It is my firm belief that a careful study of the Holy Bible from the Book of Genesis to Revelation will bring out this fact and make it very clear to anyone with an open mind. So, I can confidently say that God is well able to save (redeem) all those who put their faith in Christ, according to His plan of redemption which is revealed in the Holy Scriptures. After the fall of Adam in the Garden of Eden, God began to speak in various ways, which are recorded throughout the Scriptures, in which He outlined His plan for the redemption of mankind. I have come to firmly believe that what was laid down and accomplished for our redemption has restored Mankind into a position of dominion over the earth and legally put Satan out of business completely.

Praise God! It has pleased God that this plan of redemption should be revealed to His chosen people through the avenue of His written Word. In this volume, *Experiencing*

Introduction

Christ Jesus the Redeemer, I have attempted to present a step-by-step outline of Biblical truths, which I believe, will help the reader to gain understanding and personal experience of the realities of this redemption and as a consequence prevent the devil from having inroads into his/her life or from lording it over.

First, we must understand that the plan of redemption called for an incarnation: that is, the union of divinity with humanity in the person Jesus Christ. It is important to note that through deception, Satan became lord over the First Man, the Man from the dust, Adam. This meant that Adam and all who were born into this world after the Fall of Adam automatically come under the dominion of the devil (1 John 5:19). This was because the devil became the god of this age (2 Corinthians 4:4). So, it was necessary for God to send a Second Man, the Heavenly Man, Jesus Christ, to bring order in a world where the devil had usurped authority and power over the First Man, created chaos and had been reigning unchallenged.

The First Man was the victim in the Fall. Therefore, it took another Man, the Second Man, the Heavenly Man, Jesus Christ, to become the Victor in the redemption of Mankind. Every person that is born into this world, ruled by Satan, does not naturally know God. Therefore, I believe that the objective of Jesus' incarnation was that Mankind might be redeemed and given the opportunity to be reconciled to God, thus become children of God by receiving the nature of God (see John 1:12-13).

Secondly, it is important to know that redemption is experienced through a divine revelation of God as the only true God and believing in Jesus Christ whom He has sent. Receiving Jesus into your life as your Savior will give you the power to become a child of God. You will then receive God's divine power with which God has already provided for you everything that you may need for life and godliness. Having received these, you can, therefore, escape from the corruption that is in the world and become a partaker of the divine nature of God. You are also positioned to a place where peace and grace are multiplied to you through an intimate fellowship with God and of Jesus Christ our Lord (2 Peter 1:1-4). These things are already made yours in Christ: in whom God has prepared abundant blessings for you. But these things can become yours only through a personal relationship with the person of Jesus, who is the Redeemer.

Understand that this revelation knowledge is not just a rational knowledge, (i.e. doctrines, philosophies, and creeds, even though God has given you your mind and He does not by-passed it), but it is the reality and full truth of the Word of God revealed by the Holy Spirit. I think that Revelation knowledge in Christ is literally spiritual knowledge brought to you by divine revelation through the workings of the Holy

Introduction

Spirit. It is like God's breath and life flowing in and through you, enabling you to experience the realities of God.

Thirdly, you need to know that Satan's lordship has been overthrown, even though he is still the god of this age. The Lord Jesus, who was the seed of the woman as prophesied in the Book of Genesis, has crushed the head of the serpent. The truth is that Satan is now a defeated foe and his claims of lordship over you have been destroyed. Jesus paid the full price for you and me to be redeemed. Revelation 12:11 teaches us that the believers overcame Satan by the blood of the Lamb and by the word of their testimony, or confession.

I believe that the regular confession/declaration of God's Word will bring its working realities into my experience. This is because the Bible teaches that the worlds were framed by the word of God (Hebrews 11:3). Therefore, you may boldly confess thus: *"I am an overcomer by the blood of the Lamb and by the word of my testimony. Greater is He that is in me than he who is in the world. I am redeemed from the dominion of Satan. I can, therefore, frustrate all his assignments against my life."* (Revelation 12:11; 2 Corinthians 10:4-5; James 4:7).

Jesus is the Head of the Church; of which you are a part/member, and the devils are not. In Ephesians 1:19-23 Paul proclaims about:

"What *is* the exceeding greatness of His power towards us who believe, according to the working of His mighty power which He worked in Christ when He raised Him from the dead and seated Him at His right hand in the heavenly places, far above all principality and power and might and dominion and every name that is named, not only in this age but also in that which is to come. And He put all things under His feet and gave Him to be head over all things to the church, which is His body, the fullness of Him who fills all in all."

Therefore, Satan has no legal rule over you because you are part of the church of God of which Jesus is the Head. Hallelujah!

Please, try to pay close attention to the above truths, and let them be rooted in your consciousness. It is the truth that you know, and are grounded in, that has the power to set you free. Again, this is not just about the facts of Scriptures, but the experience of its transforming power.

Fourthly, it is important to understand that you were bought with a price. In 1 Corinthians 6:19-20, the Apostle Paul reminds us of the fact that we are the temple of the Holy Spirit which we have received from God and that we are not our own. This means that we do not own ourselves. We were

Introduction

bought with the price paid through the plan of Redemption. Because of that, we should glorify God in our bodies and spirits. Since the full price was paid and our redemption transacted, the devil's claims in our lives are now illegal and should be resisted and abhorred. We are free in Christ, but our freedom was paid for by the precious blood of Jesus.

When these simple truths find their roots in your heart and you begin to take your place and assume your rights and privileges in Christ; then God's promises will begin to manifest in your life. These promises will become true in your life because of your response by faith rooted in God's living Word. The Word of God reveals to us our inheritance in Christ. "So now brethren, I commend you to God and to the word of His grace, which is able to build you up and give you an inheritance among all those who are sanctified" (Acts 20:32).

So, as you study the Scriptures in this book, my prayer is that you may come to the full knowledge of who you are in Christ, especially in the light of your redemption which is in Christ Jesus our Lord. May you experience God's blessings of redemption in your life as Christ is revealed in you. *For Christ in you, the hope of glory*, and let all the redeemed of the Lord say, Amen!

Chapter 1

JESUS CHRIST THE SAME YESTERDAY, TODAY AND FOREVER

It was in the month of January 1997, in Yaoundé, (the capital city of the nation of Cameroon), when the German-born Evangelist, Reinhardt Bonnke, organized an evangelistic crusade that I witnessed the power of the gospel, and the authority of the name of Jesus demonstrated. The "Bonnke Crusade," as it was commonly called, was a city-wide event that shook the City of Yaoundé. There were echoes of the testimonies of salvation, miraculous healings, and deliverances. The blind received their sight, deaf ears were opened, the dumb spoke for the very first time, the lame received strength to walk and those with different kinds of diseases and sicknesses were cured and healed in the authority of the name of Jesus Christ.

At about 5:00 pm every day during the seven days of the crusade, all roads led to the *"Bonnke Crusade"* grounds where one could tell and sense the powerful presence of Jesus and the fact that He was doing good to those who were oppressed by the devil. The atmosphere was like the one described in Acts 10 where Simon Peter narrated:

> "How God anointed Jesus of Nazareth with the Holy Spirit and with power, who went about <u>doing good</u> and healing all who were oppressed by the devil, for God was with him" (Acts 10:38).

There is also an account in the Gospel of Matthew 11:2-5, where the Lord Jesus in answering the disciples of John who came inquiring of Him: "Are you the Coming One, or do we look for another" – said:

> Go and tell John the things which you hear and see: The blind see and the lame walk; the lepers are cleansed and the deaf hear; the dead are raised up and the poor have the gospel preached to them.

I could say that all the wonderful miracles that were performed in the name of Jesus during this Bonnke crusade, agreed with what the Bible teaches in Hebrews 13:8:

> "Jesus Christ, the same yesterday, today and forever."

Experiencing Christ Jesus, The Redeemer

This Scriptural verse was highlighted in my mind as the main take-home caption during this entire crusade. Yes, Jesus Christ is still saving the lost, healing the sick and setting captives free from the oppression of the devil. He is still doing "good" today. Even right now at this very moment, there are people who are being touched by His goodness and you can be one of them. Praise God! Jesus is still the same; He has not changed. Amen!

Even though this was not the first time I was witnessing a *"Bonnke Crusade."* As you may imagine, this particular crusade of January 1997 impacted me in a very special way. The first *"Bonnke Crusade"* that I had witnessed was in January of 1989 in Kumba, a town in the South West Region of Cameroon. I had just given my life over to the Lord Jesus at the time and was newly born-again. My heart was full of joy and the excitement of the new birth was welling up in me. One may say that I was fresh in the faith at the time and so a lot of what attracted me at the first crusade was largely at the emotional level.

Notable miracles also happened in the Kumba crusade just like they did in Yaoundé, but it was at the Yaoundé crusade that my attention was caught to the reality of the fact that: *"Jesus Christ is still the same yesterday, today and forever."* Jesus has not changed, and He is still doing good and healing all who are oppressed by the devil.

THE BLESSINGS OF CALVARY

Let me just share this little background information with you. In 1995, I had an encounter with the Holy Spirit during which the Lord visited me and gave me a vision of His passion from Gethsemane to Golgotha. This encounter with the Holy Spirit opened my heart to receive a revelation of what I call *the blessings of Calvary*. So, in January of 1997, even though it was over a year since this encounter with the Lord, I was just getting into the quest of finding out who Jesus was and what His mission of redemption was all about. Thus, I could say that the impact of the Yaoundé crusade in my life was greater by all proportions than that of January 1989 in Kumba. I was very impressed with the power of God that was demonstrated in the name of Jesus Christ. In Matthew 28:18-20 Jesus said:

> All authority has been given to me in heaven and on earth. Go therefore and make disciples of all nations, baptizing them in the name of the Father and of the Son and of the Holy Spirit, teaching them to observe all things that I have commanded you; and lo, I am with you always, even to the end of the earth.

It is noteworthy to see that Jesus' authority referred to in Matthew 28:18 was delegated to Him by the Father and He, in turn, delegated this authority to His disciples, and consequently to all who put their faith in the finished work of Christ on the cross. This is what is commonly called "The Great Commission." But before we can discourse about the authority of Jesus Christ and the Great Commission; I think that It is important to first find out who Jesus Christ is. Scriptures teach that He has the preeminence over all things and in Him we live, move and have our being. Amen.

A WORD OF PRAYER

Father God, thank You for Your Son, Jesus. I believe Your word which says, "Jesus Christ, the same yesterday, today and forever." Thank You, Lord Jesus, for the cross and the price you paid for my salvation: the forgiveness of sins, divine healing, and deliverance from all the oppressions of the devil. Thank You, Lord, for my redemption which is in the blood of Christ. Lord Jesus, I confess that You are the Lord and Savior over my life and that all authority in heaven and on earth is Yours, for You are Lord indeed. Amen!

Chapter 2

WHO IS JESUS CHRIST?

John the beloved disciple of Jesus opens his account of the life and ministry of Jesus Christ in the Gospel of John with this revelation:

"In the beginning was the Word, and the Word was with God, and the Word was God. He was at the beginning with God. All things were made through Him, and without Him, nothing was made that was made" (John 1:1-3).

And in verse 14 of John chapter 1, it is revealed that:

"The Word became flesh and dwelt among us, and we beheld His glory, the glory as of the only begotten of the Father, full of grace and truth."

Thus, the *"Word"* that *"was with God, and the Word"* that *"was God"* became flesh-and-blood and took on human form to live amongst men in the person of Jesus Christ.

How can this be simplified? God created the universe through *"the Word"* Who became Christ. The Word was *with* God and, at the same time, *was* Himself, God. Wow! This is a radical truth. And this truth is seen in Hebrews 1:8 where God the Father called the Son: "God."

> But to the Son, He says: "Your throne, O God, is forever and ever;"

It would be helpful for us to understand "God" here as our Creator—the divine, holy and eternally living One—as well as the *name* for that kind of being. Thus, Jesus is divine and holy in nature and eternally existed before the worlds began. The apostle Paul says that the whole divine family is named after the Father; and I believe that this includes Christ who is the Son of the Living God (Ephesians 3:14-15).

Therefore, in the beginning, was the Word (Jesus), and the Word was with God (the Father) and the Word was also named God! Of course, the Word would not be *named* God unless He was *like* the Father in image and likeness. Hebrews 1:3 attests to this when it says:

> "The Son is the radiance of God's glory and the exact representation of his being," (NIV)

So, Jesus is revealed in the New Testament Scriptures as God in the flesh. For, in 1 Timothy 3:16 the Bible says:

> "God was manifest in the flesh, justified in the Spirit, seen of angels, preached unto the Gentiles, believed on in the world, received up into glory."

There are many other references in Scriptures which attest to Jesus' divinity:

> "For unto us a child is born, unto us, a Son is given; and the government will be upon His shoulder. And His name will be called Wonderful, Counselor, Mighty God, Everlasting Father, Prince of Peace" (Isaiah 9:6).

> "Behold, the virgin shall be with child, and bear a Son, and they shall call His name Immanuel," which is translated, "God with us" (Matthew 1:23)

FORGIVENESS OF SINS

We see instances in the New Testament Scriptures where Jesus forgave the sins of men. In Mark 2:5, "He said to the paralytic, 'Son, your sins are forgiven you.'" And when the Scribes who sat amongst the people began to reason in their hearts and to think that Jesus was blaspheming, He answered and said to them:

> "But that you may know that the Son of Man has power on earth to forgive sins" (Mark 2:10).

Luke 7:48, is another instance where Jesus forgave the sins of a woman. Note that the power to forgive sins is an attribute that God alone possesses (Mark 2:6-7).

GOD ALONE DESERVES OUR WORSHIP

There are some instances in Scriptures where Jesus received worship. For instance in Matthew 2:11, where the three Wise Men from the East worshiped the baby Jesus; also in Matthew 14:33, the disciples of Jesus came and worshiped Him, saying, "Truly you are the Son of God"; and finally we see in Matthew 28 verses 9 and 17, where the risen Lord Jesus was worshiped. Thus, be mindful of the fact that Jesus had rebuked the devil on the mount of temptation, telling him that worship was an act which is reserved for God alone (Matthew 4:10). The instances just cited confirm the fact of Jesus' divinity and that He was God incarnate in the person of Jesus Christ.

Jesus Christ is the Word of God (John 1:1). The Greek word that was used here is "logos" denoting "the expression of thought—not the mere name of an object" (W.E. Vine). Jesus totally expressed the thoughts of the Father and was manifested in a physical form so that the entire world could experience God through Him (Hebrews 1:3).

JESUS CHRIST'S INCARNATION

Jesus Christ, "Who, being in very nature God, did not consider equality with God something to be grasped, but made himself nothing, taking the very nature of a servant, being made in human likeness. And being found in appearance as a man, he humbled himself and became obedient to death— even death on a cross!" (Philippians. 2:6-8).

In presenting the incarnate Jesus, we need to consider the fact that, Jesus did not demand or cling to His rights as God but laid aside His Divine rights and privileges in order to take the form of a servant and be made in the likeness of men. He further humbled Himself by becoming obedient to the Father, even to the point of death.

This was the supreme sacrifice that identified Jesus totally with humanity and enabled God to redeem mankind. By taking on human form and dying a criminal's death upon the cross, Jesus Christ fulfilled the Old Testament law of Deuteronomy 21:22-23 which says:

> If a man guilty of a capital offense is put to death and his body is hung on a tree, you must not leave his body on the tree overnight. Be sure to bury him that same day, because anyone who is hung on a tree is under God's curse.

And in so doing He bore our curse in His own body. This was the price He paid to redeem us from the curse of the law and therefore opened wide God's blessing of justification through faith in Christ and the promise of His Holy Spirit (See Galatians 3:13-14).

Therefore, it is necessary for every Christian to understand that God's plan for our redemption called for an incarnation; which was the union of divinity with humanity in Jesus Christ. I believe this to be the fundamental revelation knowledge that empowers every believer to escape the corruption that is in the world and to be partakers of the divine nature in Christ (2 Peter 1:3-4). That is, Christ in you the hope of glory! (Colossians 1:27). The Bible teaches that all have sinned and fallen short of the glory of God. Thus, there was no one without sin before God on earth. God had given the earth to Mankind as an inheritance, and Satan through deception and sin succeeded to steal it way. Mankind was robbed of the glory of God and trapped in the principle of sin and death. Therefore, there was a need for a savior, and there was no one to fulfill that role. So, God had to become the Son of Man. He had to be born into the earth in order to save mankind. When Jesus did that and became our Savior, every born-again believer in Christ can now receive the same nature that Jesus had when he walked the earth in flesh and blood and can enjoy the blessed inheritance of the Sons of God (John 1:16). And as Jesus is, so are we in this world (1 John 4:17).

GOD'S LOVE GIFT - JESUS CHRIST

In my quest to understand who Jesus is, I have come to see Him as God's *"ultimate Gift of Himself"* for the redemption of a hopelessly lost world that was under the sway of the devil and his associates. God demonstrated His love for us in that while we were yet in our sins, Christ died for us (Romans 5:8).

It is really much more than Jesus dying on the cross for the sins of the world. He came for the restoration of that which was lost. Jesus said, *"For the Son of man came to seek and to save what was lost."* We have traditionally interpreted and applied these words of Jesus only to the salvation of perishing men from the flames of hell. But He left His eternal glory, came to earth in a flesh and blood suit, demonstrated the love of the Father towards fallen humanity, took upon Himself all the sins, curses, sicknesses and diseases of the entire world; He was made sin for our sake, then went to the cross and died a criminals death so that we can be redeemed and that we may receive the power to become God's children. Here is where I believe is the premise for our invitation into experiencing Christ Jesus the Redeemer.

> "But as many, as received Him, to them he gave the right to become children of God, to those who believe in His name" (John 1:12)

A WORD OF PRAYER

Father God, thank You for the Lord Jesus. I believe Your word, which teaches that Jesus Christ was God manifested in the flesh. He is the very image of Your person. Thank You, Lord Jesus, for going to the cross and for the price you paid for my redemption. Lord, I declare my love for you. I praise and worship You, Lord Jesus, for my redemption that was purchased with Your blood, the precious blood of Christ. Lord Jesus, I confess that You are the Lord and Savior over my life, my Redeemer. Indeed, all authority in heaven and on earth is Yours, for You are Lord. Amen!

Chapter 3

THE NAME OF JESUS

The Name of Jesus was first revealed to Mary by the angel Gabriel and later to Joseph through a dream by an angel of God. While Joseph was contemplating a secrete divorce with Mary his betrothed wife, God intervened and told him not to be afraid to take Mary as his wife. An account of this story is recorded for us in the Gospel of Matthew.

> "Now the birth of Jesus Christ was as follows: After His mother, Mary was betrothed to Joseph, before they came together, she was found with child of the Holy Spirit. Then Joseph her husband, being a just *man,* and not wanting to make her a public example, was minded to put her away secretly. But while he thought about these things, behold, an angel of the Lord appeared to him in a dream, saying,

> 'Joseph, son of David, do not be afraid to take to you Mary your wife, for that which is conceived in her, is of the Holy Spirit. And she will bring forth a son, and you shall call His name JESUS, for He will save His people from their sins.'" (Matthew 1:18-21)

Our attention needs to be drawn to the fact that the Name of JESUS is synonymous with "Savior of His people." So, the angel instructed Joseph to name Him JESUS because He will save His people from their sins. He identified Himself with our humanity so as to become our Savior. This truth is further verified in Acts 4:12 where Peter said:

> "Salvation is found in no one else, for there is no other name under heaven given to men by which we must be saved." (NIV)

The name JESUS in New Testament Greek is "Iesous" (e-ay-soos'). But the origin of Jesus' name can be traced back to the Hebrew name of "Joshua," pronounced *Yehowshuwa* (yeh-ho-shoo'-ah); or *Yehoshua*. The name Joshua means "Yahweh saves" or "Yahweh is Savior." It is important to say that, the Name of JESUS was not decided upon in an arbitrary fashion as many children's names are. JESUS' name was given based upon His mission in life, and His mission was determined from the foundation of the world— "the Lamb of God slain from the foundation of the world." He was to save us from our sins through a onetime sacrifice of Himself for the redemption of all people and for all time. The significance of the Name of JESUS does not end with His mission on earth. It is also found in the fact that the name JESUS and YAHWEH are the same.

Let us investigate this together.

On the day of Pentecost, while Peter was addressing the crowd that gathered after the outpouring of the Holy Spirit, he quoted Joel 2:32 and said:

> "And it shall come to pass that whosoever calls on the name of the LORD [Yahweh] shall be saved" (Acts 2:21)

After the healing of the lame man from birth at the gate called Beautiful, Peter, filled with the Holy Spirit, while addressing the Sanhedrin said:

> "Let it be known to you all, and to all the people of Israel, that by the name of Jesus Christ of Nazareth, whom you crucified, whom God raised from the dead, by Him this man stands here before you whole" (Acts 4:10).

Peter further went on to say that:

> "Nor is there salvation in any other, for there is no other name under heaven given among men by which we must be saved" (Acts 4:12).

If salvation is found only in the name of Jesus, for there is no other name under heaven by which we must be saved, then the name of the LORD [Yahweh] spoken of in Acts 2:21 must be the same name that is spoken of in Acts 4:12.

This can further be verified in Romans 10:9-10 where the Bible says,

> "That if you confess with your mouth the Lord Jesus and believe in your heart that God raised Him from the dead, <u>you shall be saved</u>. For with the heart one believes unto righteousness, and with the mouth, confession is made unto salvation."

And in Romans 10:13 the Bible goes on to say,

> "For whoever calls on the name of the LORD [Yahweh] <u>shall be saved</u>."

You see, the one true God, who alone stretched out the heavens, and spread out the earth by Himself, came to earth in human form in the person of Jesus Christ. Salvation is found in calling on the name of Jesus because Jesus Christ is LORD [YAHWEH].

NAME ABOVE ALL NAMES

In John 17:11-12 (NIV), while the Lord Jesus was praying for His disciples, He said, "Holy Father, protect them by the power of Your Name-- the Name You gave Me.

...While I was with them, I protected them and kept them safe by that Name You gave Me."

It is acknowledged that the Name of Jesus was given to Him by the Father. Philippians 2:9 says, "God also has highly exalted Him and given Him the Name which is above every name." But Jesus' language in John 17:11 revealed the fact that the name the Father gave Him was the very name of the Father. He said, "...*protect them by the power of Your Name– the Name you gave me.*" If the Name of Jesus is "the Name which is above every name, that at the Name of Jesus every knee should bow, of those in heaven, and of those on the earth, and of those under the earth." Then the Name of Jesus must surely be of equal authority to that of the Father. Or better still, it is the same Name as the Father's. The Name of the Father cannot possibly bow at the Name of Jesus, right?

In Psalms 138:2, King David, inspired by the Holy Spirit, proclaimed:

> "I will worship toward Your holy temple and praise Your Name for Your lovingkindness and Your truth; for You have magnified Your word above all Your Name."

Think about this for a moment.

The Bible teaches in Revelation 19:13 that JESUS is called the Word of God. If the Word of God has been magnified above all the Name of Yahweh. Therefore, we can confidently conclude that all the names of God revealed in the Old Testament Scriptures are all embodied in the Name of JESUS which is the Name that is above every name.

POWER IN THE NAME OF JESUS

Jesus Christ has given all who trust in Him the right and authority to use His name. This means that all believers in Christ have been given the power of attorney. Legally speaking, the power of attorney is the authority to act on another person's behalf, at their request. It is authorization given by one person permitting another to act on his behalf.

I remember an incident when I had to sign the power of attorney over to my wife. It was in September of 2009 after I was involved in a car accident. The car I was driving in was wrecked, (that is, it was damaged beyond repairs), and towed away while I was rushed to the hospital by an ambulance. On the following day, while I was still in the hospital, my wife went to the lot where my car was parked with my ID card and the title certificate of the car, but she was denied access to the car. Even though she got me on the phone, and I talked with the manager of the tow company to let her collect my personal effects from the car, she was not allowed access to the car. The reason he gave was that: though she was my wife, her name was not on the title certificate of the car. To cut a long story short, she was only given access to the car after I had signed a notarized note authorizing her to act on my behalf. She had to present a legal written document signed by me with her name on it, showing that she could act on my behalf.

It is the same thing for every Christian. You see because we are joint-heirs with Christ (and our names are written in the Lamb's Book of Life), He has given us the power of attorney-- full authority-- to do and command in His name. This power of attorney we are talking about is not just a promise, but it is a legal written document— God's written Word which is settled in Heaven. Therefore, we can say and prove that: "It is written." Jesus said:

> "And whatever you ask in My Name, that I will do, that the Father may be glorified in the Son. If you ask anything in My Name, I will do it." (John 14:13, 14)

> "Whatever you ask the Father in My Name He will give you. Until now you have asked nothing in My Name. Ask, and you will receive, that your joy may be full." (John 16:23, 24)

I will take this opportunity to caution you that the Name of Jesus Christ is not a magic formula. The power of His Name is not even in saying the Name JESUS, but it is in the nature of our relationship with Him. It is in our understanding and believing in all that the Name of Jesus Christ signifies. His Name represents all of His finished work on the cross, fulfilling God's plan of redemption and salvation, victory over sin, death, and overthrowing the devil's entire realm. When the name of Jesus Christ is invoked/called on, it carries with it all of the authority and power of the Kingdom of Heaven and the majesty of its King. God raised Jesus from the dead, elevated Him to His right hand, and gave Him a Name above *"every name that is named, not only in this age but also in that which is to come"* (Ephesians 1:21).

Philippians 2:9, 10 declares:

> "God also has highly exalted Him and given Him the Name, which is above every name, that at the Name of Jesus every knee should bow, of those in heaven, and of those on earth, and of those under the earth."

ALL THINGS ARE SUBJECT TO THE NAME OF JESUS

Regarding Jesus, Hebrews 2:8 teaches that:

> For in that He put all in subjection under him, he left nothing that is not put under him.

I attended a seminar by Professor Joseph T. Mbafor, International President of Christian Missionary Fellowship International and Associated Churches, with headquarters in Yaoundé, Cameroon. At this seminar, he presented the following as those things which are subject to the Name of Jesus.

- Satan and all of hell
- All principalities and powers
- All human kingdoms and governments
- The world's systems and its glory
- Money and wealth
- Every human being and authority
- Every sickness and disease
- All viruses, fungi, and bacteria
- Every bird, animal and sea creatures
- The weather, the seas, and the oceans
- All crops, and trees
- All circumstances of life

In this same seminar, Professor Mbafor further explained that the Names of Jesus should be used by Spirit filed believers who:

- Know, love and adore Him
- Obey Him and are guided only by His Spirit.
- Server Him and do everything for His glory.

SOME INSTANCES IN WHICH THE NAME OF JESUS WAS USED IN THE BOOK OF ACTS

We see in Acts chapter 2, where after Peter's powerful sermon on the day of Pentecost, the people were deeply moved, and inquired, "What do we do?"

Peter answered:

> "Repent and let every one of you be baptized in the name of Jesus Christ for the remission of sins; and you shall receive the gift of the Holy Spirit" (Acts 2:38).

Another instance where the power of the name of Jesus was used, was at the gate Beautiful when Peter and John were going into the temple; a lame man asked for alms, and Peter said:

> "Silver and gold, I do not have, but what I do have I give you: In the name of Jesus Christ of Nazareth, rise up and walk" (Acts 3:6).

As a result, this man was miraculously healed and made whole. And when Peter was questioned about this healing miracle, he was very bold in defending the name of Jesus and all it stands for. He said:

> "Let it be known to you all, and to all the people of Israel, that by the name of Jesus Christ of Nazareth, whom you crucified, whom God raised from the dead, by Him this man stands here before you whole. Nor is there salvation in any other, for there is no other name under heaven given among men by which we must be saved" (Acts 4:10, 12).

This third incident happened in the city of Philippi when a slave girl who had a spirit of divination followed Paul and his team shouting,

"These men are servants of the Most-High God, who are telling you the way to be saved" (Acts 16:18).

She continued in this way for many days until Paul became disturbed and turned and said to the spirit:

"In the Name of Jesus Christ, I command you to come out of her!" At that moment the spirit left her (Acts 16:16-18).

The fourth incident in Acts 19:11-20 illustrates the abuse of the Name of the Lord by people who do not know and depend on Him as Paul did. That Name is not a mere Name that is used by witches and sorcerers as magical incantations! Even demons fear that Name and can react as the demoniac who alone beat and disgraced the seven sons of "Priest" Sceva.

It is by faith in this name above all names, the name of Jesus Christ, that people are saved, set free from bondage, healed of sicknesses and diseases, and that miracles are worked. There is no other Name under heaven more powerful or more significant, and this is a dynamic reality that all believers can believe in and have complete confidence.

AUTHORITY IN THE NAME OF JESUS

The authority that all believers have in using the name of Jesus is not for us to wrestle against flesh and blood, but against principalities, against powers, against the rulers of the

The Name of Jesus

darkness of this age, against spiritual hosts of wickedness in the heavenly places (Ephesians 6:12). Therefore, a believer may exercise authority in the name of Jesus against any spiritual force in opposition to the Lordship of Jesus. So, it is with this understanding that I share the following testimony with you.

> "I was in a meeting in Los Angeles on one occasion. An old black man was conducting the services. He had the funniest vocabulary. But I want to tell you, there were doctors, lawyers, and professors listening to marvelous things coming from his lips. It was not what he said in words; it was what he said from his spirit to my heart that showed me he had more of God in his life than any man I had ever met up to that time. It was God in him who was attracting people."
>
> "One man insisted on getting up and talking every little while. Some people have a mania for talking. The old black brother endured it for a long time. Finally, the fellow got up again, and the old man stuck his finger out and said, "In the Name of Jesus Christ, sit down!" The man did not sit down. He fell down. And his friends carried him out. That is only one of the living facts of what Christianity is: the divine power of Jesus Christ by the Holy Spirit, filling a man's soul and body, flashing through his nature like a holy flame, accomplishing the will of God." (John G. Lake, *Adventures in God*)

"These things I have written to you who believe in the Name of the Son of God, that you may know that you have eternal life and that you may continue to believe in the Name of the Son of God." (1 John 5:13)

A WORD OF PRAYER

Father God, thank You for Your Son, Jesus. I believe in the name of Jesus, the Name that is above all names. Thank You, Lord, for the authority which I have in the Name of Jesus. The Name which is far above all principalities and powers, all thrones and dominions, and every name that is named, not only in this age but also in that which is to come. Thank You, Lord, for my redemption that is ratified in the blood of Christ. Lord Jesus, I confess that You are the Lord and Savior over my life. I believe that all authority in heaven and on earth is Yours and that you have given me the right to use your name for Your glory. Thank You, LORD. Amen!

Chapter 4

THE ON-GOING MINISTRY OF JESUS

We are told in the Gospels that the earthly ministry of Jesus lasted just for about three and a half years, but it was a ministry with a very far-reaching impact. Everyone who encountered Jesus was radically impacted by His Ministry. His public ministry impacted the entire nation of Israel: cities, villages, and communities. He also touched the lives of many people at a very personal level. Jesus' ministry was centered on the preaching and the demonstration of the kingdom of God. "Your kingdom come and Your will be done on earth as in heaven," could be derived as the overriding purpose in describing the ministry of Jesus from start to finish. I believe that there was no other overriding subject on His mind than that of the kingdom of God. Jesus was "Immanuel", that is, "God with us." Therefore,

> Jesus began to preach and to say, "Repent, for the kingdom of heaven is at hand" (Matthew. 4:17)

> He said... "I must preach the kingdom of God to other cities also because for this purpose I have been sent." (Luke 4:43)

In the account of the Life and Ministry of Jesus which has been recorded for us by Luke the Beloved Physician; he investigated about:

> ...all that Jesus began both to do and teach, until the day in which he was taken up after He through the Holy Spirit had given commandments to the apostles whom He had chosen, ...and speaking of the things pertaining to the kingdom of God. (Acts 1:1-3)

LIKE FATHER, LIKE SON

Hebrews 1:3 teaches that Jesus was the express image of the person of God. Thus, Jesus totally expressed the thoughts of the Father and was manifested in a physical form so that the entire world could experience the Kingdom of God through Him. Jesus said:

> "When you lift up the Son of Man, then you will know that I am *He* and *that* I do nothing of Myself; but as My Father taught Me, I speak these things. And He who sent Me is

with Me. The Father has not left Me alone, for I always do those things that please Him." (John 8:28-29)

Anyone seeking to know, and experience God ought to look at His Son– Jesus Christ. For Jesus said,

"If you had known Me, you would have known My Father also." (John 14:7)

"Most assuredly, I say to you, the Son can do nothing of Himself, but what He sees the Father do; for whatever He does, the Son also does in like manner. For the Father loves the Son and shows Him all things that He Himself does; ...." (John 5:19-20)

Thus, we confirm that Jesus was the expression of God's thought. He only spoke what He heard from the Father and did only what He saw the Father doing. He was the image of the invisible God and the brightness of the Father's glory.

FOUNDATION OF JESUS' MINISTRY

The word foundation is here employed to portray the principles on which Jesus based His earthly ministry. Though He ministered under the Old Covenant (the Law of Moses); the ministry of Jesus was very different from that of every other religious leader before Him. We see in the Gospel of John 1:14, where we are told that He was "full of grace and truth." And it is also recorded that the company of angels that sang to announce the birth of Jesus said: "Glory to God in the highest, and on earth peace, goodwill towards men." Therefore, the Bible goes on to teach that:

> "God was in Christ reconciling the world to Himself, not imputing their trespasses to them...." (2 Cor. 5:19)

I believe that the above verse of Scripture reveals the underlying principle upon which Jesus operated on the earth. That is, *that God was at work in Christ reconciling the world to Himself, not counting men's sins against them* (NIV). Jesus' own words in John 3:17, (in which He said, *"For God did not send His Son into the world to condemn the world, but that the world through him might be saved"),* further confirms my belief. So, with this foundation in mind, we would explore the ministry of Jesus as it is recorded for us in the Gospels.

Therefore, the Lord Jesus began His earthly ministry by declaring in Luke 4:18-19 that:

> "The Spirit of the LORD is upon Me, because He has anointed Me to preach the gospel to the poor; He has sent Me to heal the brokenhearted, to proclaim liberty to the captives and recovery of sight to the blind, to set at liberty those who are oppressed; to proclaim the acceptable year of the LORD."

In Acts chapter 10 while Peter was at the house of Cornelius; he described the ministry of Jesus as *"The word which God sent to the children of Israel, preaching peace through Jesus Christ"* and narrated: "How God anointed Jesus of Nazareth with the Holy Spirit and with power, who went about doing good and healing those who were oppressed of the devil, for God was with Him" (Acts 10:38).

A WOMAN HEALED FROM A SPIRIT OF INFIRMITY

"Now He was teaching in one of the synagogues on the Sabbath. And behold, there was a woman who had a spirit of infirmity eighteen years and was bent over and could in no way raise herself up. But when Jesus saw her, He called her to Him and said to her, "Woman, you are loosed from your infirmity." And He laid His hands on her, and immediately she was made straight, and glorified God."

"But the ruler of the synagogue answered with indignation because Jesus had healed on the Sabbath; and he said to the crowd, "There are six days on which men ought to work; therefore come and be healed on them, and not on the Sabbath day.""

"The Lord then answered him and said, "Hypocrite! Does not each of you on the Sabbath loose his ox or donkey from the stall, and lead it away to water it? So, ought not this woman, being a daughter of Abraham, whom Satan has bound—think of it—for eighteen years, be loosed from this bond on the Sabbath." And when he said these things, all

His adversaries were put to shame; and all the multitude rejoiced for all the glorious things that were done by Him." (Luke 13:10-17)

We can see from the healing of this woman from the spirit of infirmity, that God was with Jesus of Nazareth as He went about doing good and healing all who were oppressed of the devil. Jesus has not changed, and He deeply cares about you, just like He did for this woman. He is able to heal you from any oppression of the devil. Yes, He does heal and deliver because He is good, and He came to do you good. Say Amen!

MINISTRY OF RECONCILIATION

We have seen that Jesus was full of grace and truth and that the purpose for which He was sent by the Father was to proclaim the good news of the kingdom of God: preaching the peace and goodwill of heaven towards men. And, that God was at work in Christ reconciling the world unto Himself, not counting their sins against them (2 Corinthians 5:19).

Now then, consider the fact that John the Baptist had introduced Jesus as the Lamb of God who takes away the sin of the world. Let us pay attention to the present tense in this statement: *The Lamb of God who takes away the sin of the world* (John 1:29). This was so because Jesus was the Lamb of God that was slain from the foundation of the world

(Revelation 13:8). This was a settled fact in the realms of the spirit; that is, that the Lord Jesus had paid for the sin of the whole world. It could be likened to a credit that was imputed on Jesus' account. Therefore, He was manifested to let people experience the benefits of this spiritual transaction of the Kingdom of God on earth. Thus, Jesus came in the flesh in order to destroy and eradicate the power of sin, which is the power through which the devil gained access and authority in the earth realm and over the lives of men. For the devil was the author of sin. The Holy Bible teaches that "For this reason, the Son of God was manifested that He might destroy the works of the devil" (1 John 3:8).

Yes, Jesus was manifested to deal with the sin problem of humanity in order to manifest the Kingdom of Heaven on earth amongst men. This opened the way for people to experience, in Christ Jesus, the freedom from sin and its oppressive consequences.

JESUS FORGIVES AND HEALS

> "And again, He entered Capernaum after some days, and it was heard that He was in the House. Immediately many gathered together so that there was no longer room to receive them, not even near the door. And He preached the word to them. Then they came to Him, bringing a paralytic who was carried by four men. And when they could not

come near Him because of the crowd, they uncovered the roof where He was. So, when they had broken through, they let down the bed on which the paralytic was lying."

"When Jesus saw their faith, He said to the paralytic, "Son, your sins are forgiven you"

"And the scribes were sitting there and reasoning in their hearts," Why does this man speak blasphemies like this? Who can forgive sins but God alone?"

"But immediately, when Jesus perceived in His spirit that they reasoned thus within themselves, He said to them, "Why do you reason about these things in your hearts? Which is easier, to say to the paralytic, 'Your sins are forgiven you,' or to say 'Arise, take up your bed and walk? But that you may know that the Son of Man has power on the earth to forgive sins'– He said to the paralytic, "I say to you, arise take up your bed and go to your house." Immediately he arose, took up the bed, and went out in the presence of them all, so that all were amazed and glorified God, saying, "We never saw anything like this!" (Mark 2:1-12)

Jesus' ministry to this paralytic man was consistent with all the scriptures that we have seen while we were trying to establish the foundation of His earthly ministry. Jesus was manifested to destroy the power of sin and its inroads into the lives of people, (sickness and diseases, oppression of the devil

Experiencing Christ Jesus, The Redeemer

and every work of darkness). He came in the flesh and dwelt amongst us; full of grace and truth. Since He was the Lamb of God that was slain from the foundation of the world, He could proclaim the fact that the sins of the paralytic are forgiven; and because he was forgiven, God's will which was settled in heaven, (which is that he should prosper and be in health even as his soul prospers), could now be experienced by him.

Now, the Scribes were sitting there and reasoning in their hearts, thinking that Jesus was blaspheming as He said, "Son, your sins are forgiving you." The Bible tells us that Jesus in reply said to them: "But that you may know that the Son of Man has power on the earth to forgive sins" – He said to the paralytic, "I say to you, arise take up your bed and go to your house." Anyone who truly believes in Jesus has been given the right to receive the forgiveness of their sins and the healing of their bodies.

I want you to take note that Jesus did not make a distinction between the forgiveness of this man's sins and his healing. Also, remember that Jesus did nothing on His own authority; God was with Him. He only did and said those things which He heard and saw His Father doing. So, Jesus has not changed; He is the same yesterday, today and forever. If Jesus has declared that your sins are forgiven, then sickness and diseases have no legal place in your body. They must go,

The On-Going Ministry of Jesus

for their power has been broken and their legal rights removed. Therefore, seek first the forgiveness that is being offered by Jesus. He is the Lamb of God that takes away the sins of the world.

So, with these truths in mind, let us take a look at another person whom Jesus ministered to. Come with me as I look at the story of the man healed at the pool of Bethesda.

> "Now a certain man was there who had an infirmity thirty-eight years. When Jesus saw him lying there and knew that he already had been in that condition a long time, He said to him, "Do you want to be made well?"
>
> The sick man answered Him, "Sir, I have no man to put me into the pool when the water is stirred up; but while I am coming, another steps down before me."
>
> Jesus said to him, "Rise, take up your bed and walk." And immediately the man was made well, took up his bed, and walked. (John 5:5-8)

The man at the pool of Bethesda was healed by Jesus, and he did not even know the person who had healed him. His healing was not the result of his own efforts in prayer neither was it that of his friends. He had no strength to go into the pool when the water was stirred, and neither was there anyone to assist him. Apparently, his sick condition was a result of some personal sin in his life. But Jesus healed him all the same without making any mention of his sin. Jesus was doing good and healing him of the oppression of the devil who is the author of sin. But for him to continue benefiting from the grace of God that was manifested towards him, Jesus had to share the truth with him. The Bible says:

> Afterward, Jesus found him in the temple, and said to him, "See, you have been made well. Sin no more, lest a worse thing come upon you." (John 5:14)

It is very important that you understand that: sin is an offense towards God from which you must repent and turn away, and that: sin is also the avenue through which the kingdom of darkness gains inroads into the lives of men. Sin gives the devil a legal right to work his death into your life. This is because every time you sin, you yield yourself to him – that is, the devil who is the author and copyright owner of all sin.

> "Do you not know that to whom you present yourselves, slaves, to obey, you are that one's slaves whom you obey, whether of sin leading to death or of obedience leading to righteousness?" (Romans 6:16).

BE OF GOOD CHEER

"Jesus Christ is the same yesterday, today and forever." (Hebrews. 13:8) God is no respecter of persons; and what He has done for one He is able to do for another, even you. Be of good cheer my dear friend, because something good is about to happen to you. Jesus is still "doing good and healing all who are oppressed of the devil."

I have seen God heal and deliver people who were in hopeless medical situations. I am reminded of a young man by name Floyd who came to us for prayers because the doctors could not help him. His kidneys were shutting down and his liver was also being affected as a result. I told him that Jesus was able to heal him if only he could believe. He said with tears in his eyes, "I believe, please pray for me." And we prayed for him to be healed in the name of Jesus. At the end of the ministration through prayers, I advised him to go to the doctor for medical check-up and to come back to us with the results. After about three weeks he came back with a testimony of God's merciful miraculous healing power in his life. The doctor's report showed that his kidneys were brand new. Without a doubt, he had received two brand new kidneys through the prayer of faith in the name of Jesus. Praise the Lord! Jesus is still in the business of doing good and healing the oppressed.

POWER BELONGS TO THE LORD

Here again, is another thrilling testimony of the continuous ministry and goodness of Jesus in the lives of men. This is being quoted as it was recorded by John G. Lake in his book: "Adventures in God."

"I was sitting one day in the home of the DeValeras in Krugersdorp, South Africa, when a man arrived who had traveled all over the country. He had been following me from place to place, trying to catch up with me. He suffered a sunstroke which had affected his mind and he also had developed a large cancer."

"He came into the house and proved to be a friend of the family. In a little while, a six-year-old child who had been sitting near me went across the room, climbed on the man's knees, put her hands on the cancer on his face, and prayed. I saw the cancer wither. In half an hour, the thing had disappeared. The wound was still there, but in a few days, it was healed."

"After the child had laid her hands on the top of his head, he arose, saying, "Oh! The fire that has been in my brain has gone out," and his mind was normal."

"Power belongeth unto God. Psalms 62: 11. The simplest soul can touch God and live in the very presence of God and in His power. It is almost a sadness to my soul that men should be astonished and surprised at ordinary, tangible evidence of the power of God."

THE MAN JESUS

The below insert was written by "Daddy" Atogho, (as he was fondly known by members of Christian Missionary Fellowship International & Associated Churches), who wrote the forward to this book. This was a handwritten note which he gave to me after he had reviewed and proofread this chapter on "The On-Going Ministry of Jesus." He wanted me to look into these areas of Jesus' on-going ministry to the believer. So, I have inserted it here, just as it was written:

> "Talking of that power, our minds go back to this Jesus who is not only our Only Way, our Only Truth, and our Only Life that comes from God., but He is also our High Priest, our Surety in all things divine and eternal."

> "As our High Priest, He entered the Throne Room of grace and offered His own blood and obtained eternal redemption for us. The Father could not and cannot reject His own offer, His own solution, His own price for our redemption."

> "As our Mediator, sent by the Father, He is the facilitator of our reunion and reconciliation with God. No one else could be acceptable to the Father."

> "As our Intercessor, He does not only provide His own blood to cleanse all confessed sin, He prays for us, God's

children, pleading for the renewing of our minds and protection from demons which persecute us for having received God's righteousness."

"As our Advocate, appointed by the Father to be with Him and defend us, we should gladly turn to Jesus, confess any blemish that tarnishes our fellowship with God, and be sure that our Advocate pleads our cause and receives the Father's forgiveness, sanctification, and restoration."

"As we abide and dwell in the Lord Jesus, and He abides and dwells in us, He becomes and remains our Surety for eternal redemption and a practically victorious Christian life." (By David Atogho, 1936-2017)

IT IS TIME TO PRAY NOW

Heavenly Father, I thank you for Jesus Christ, who is the Son of the living God. I thank You for His ministry which has not changed because He is the same yesterday, today and forever. Lord, I repent of any sins in my life or my ancestor's lives that have given place for the devil to come in and produce his cursed works of death in my life. I repent of all disobedience, rebellion, perversion, witchcraft, idolatry, lust, adultery, fornication, mistreatment of others, unforgiveness, hatred, bitterness, murder, cheating, lying, hypocrisy, sorcery, divination, and occult involvement, and I ask for Your forgiveness and cleansing through the blood of the Lord Jesus.

I confess that all my sins have been forgiven and remitted because of the shed blood of Jesus on the cross. Therefore, in the name of Jesus, I set myself loose from every inroad of the devil in my life which came about as a result of all disobedience and rebellion to the word of God. In the name of Jesus, I command sickness and disease to go from my body. In the name of Jesus, I command my body to be healed and made whole. I declare that my body has been healed because Jesus has paid the price for my healing. For by the stripe of Jesus I have been healed. So, body, be healed in Jesus' mighty Name.

Thank you, Lord Jesus, for Your healing power which is at work right now in my body. I believe and receive my healing now, in Jesus' name. Amen!

Chapter 5

REDEMPTION IN CHRIST

Redemption is a noun that is derived from the verb *"to redeem."* The verb *to redeem* is defined by The American Heritage® Dictionary of the English Language, as follows:

1. To recover possession or ownership of by payment of a price or service; to regain.
2. To pay off (a promissory note, for example)
3. To turn in (coupons, for example) and receive something in exchange.
4. To set free upon payment of a ransom, to rescue.
5. To save from a state of sinfulness and its consequences.

Therefore, when we discuss redemption in Christ, we are talking about how Christ Jesus—the Son of the Living God—finished His work as our Redeemer to acquire salvation for us through His shed blood on the cross of Calvary. But before we delve into redemption in Christ, I would love for you to come with me as we look at Israel's redemption from Pharaoh's tyranny. I believe that the redemption of the Israelites from Egyptian bondage provides for us a good parallel to the Christian's redemption in Christ.

ISRAEL'S REDEMPTION FROM EGYPTIAN BONDAGE

The concept of redemption was first revealed in the Bible as it is recorded for us in the book of Exodus. Pharaoh had succeeded to enslave innocent Israelites through conspiracies and shrewd dealings and had *"set taskmasters over the Israelites to afflict them with their burdens" (Exodus 1:11)*. So, the Israelites were enslaved and subjected to forced labor, and were in Egyptian bondage for over four hundred years when God sent Moses to announce to them their redemption:

> And God spoke to Moses and said to him: I am Yahweh. I appeared to Abraham, to Isaac, and to Jacob, as God Almighty, but by my Name Yahweh, I was not known to them. I have also established my covenant with them, to give them the land of Canaan, the land of their pilgrimage, in which they were strangers. And I have also heard the groaning of the children of Israel whom the Egyptians keep in bondage, and I have remembered my covenant. Therefore, say to the children of Israel, I am Yahweh; I will

bring you out from under the burdens of the Egyptians, I will <u>redeem</u> you with an outstretched arm and with great judgments. I will take you as my people and I will be your God. Then you shall know that I am Yahweh your God who brings you out from under the burdens of the Egyptians. And I will bring you into the land which I swore to give to Abraham, Isaac, and Jacob; and I will give it to you as a heritage: I am Yahweh. (Exodus 6:2-8)

From the above Biblical passage, God spoke to Moses and made the following declarations:

1. I am Yahweh, the Eternal Omnipotent and faithful One. I appeared to Abraham, to Isaac, and to Jacob, as God Almighty, but by My Name Yahweh, I was not known to them.
2. I have also established My sworn covenant with Abraham, Isaac, and Jacob to give them the land of Canaan, formerly the land of their pilgrimage as a heritage.
3. I have heard the groaning of the children of Israel and I have remembered My sworn covenant.

It is significant to note here that God considered the redemption of the children of Israel to be His personal affair. Therefore, He begins His conversation with Moses with the revelation of His personal Name, Yahweh or Jehovah, the Omnipotent and Unchangeable I AM. He was personally getting involved with the plight of the Israelites, and that was all because of a covenant He had made and sworn with Abraham, Isaac, and Jacob. It was time for God to fulfill His covenant with them. Thus, I believe: *God is Redeemer and a covenant-keeping God*, and that is the significance of His personal Name, Yahweh. This fact can be verified in what God said to the Israelites through Moses:

> "Then you shall know that I am Yahweh your God who brings you out from under the burdens of the Egyptians. And I will bring you into the land which I swore to give to Abraham, Isaac, and Jacob; and I will give it to you as a heritage: I am Yahweh." (Exo 6:6-8)

So, God was introducing Himself to Moses and the Israelites as Yahweh, a Name bearing attributes that were unknown to Abraham, Isaac, and Jacob; but were being revealed at this time when He was about to fulfill His covenant with them. He said to Moses,

> "I have also heard the groaning of the children of Israel whom the Egyptians keep in bondage, and I have remembered my covenant" (Exo. 6:5).

Therefore, it could be said that: because of God's sworn covenant with Abraham, Isaac, and Jacob, God sent Moses to the children of Israel to declare to them the following:

1. I am Yahweh. I will bring you out from under the burdens of the Egyptians.
2. I will rescue you from their bondage.
3. I will redeem you with an outstretched arm and spectacular judgments.
4. I will take you as my people and I will be your God.
5. I will bring you into the land which I swore to give to Abraham, Isaac, and Jacob.
6. I will give the land of the Canaanites to you as a heritage. I am Yahweh.

According to what is recorded in Exodus 6:5, we can see that the groaning of the children of Israel whom the Egyptians kept in bondage had reached the ears of God and He was concerned not just about their freedom, but with His own obligation to respect the covenant He had sworn with Abraham. Therefore, it was necessary for God to reveal Himself more to Moses and to the children of Israel, insisting on the covenant He had sworn with Abraham in Genesis chapter 15 and later repeated to Isaac and Jacob.

You see, God does nothing in the earth realm except by first speaking it forth. This is because He is *"upholding all things by the word of His power"* (Heb. 1:3). If God has spoken a word over your life and that word amounts to an oat by Him, you can stand in faith on that word in earnest expectation for its fulfillment. God watches over His word to fulfill it. God's word cannot fall to the ground. "For as the rain comes down, and the snow from heaven and do not return there, but water the earth, and make it bring forth and bud, that it may give seed to the sower and bread to the eater, so shall My word be that goes forth from My mouth; it shall not return to Me void, but it shall accomplish what I please, and it shall prosper in the thing for which I sent it" (Isaiah 55:10-11).

YAHWEH, THE REDEEMER OF ISRAEL

God redeemed the children of Israel from under the Egyptian bondage with an outstretched arm and great demonstrations of His power and therefore, fulfilled His covenant with Abraham, Isaac, and Jacob. Note that the grounds on which God stood to free His people were the obligation to the fulfillment of His sworn word to their forefathers resulting in spectacular judgments on stubborn Egypt.

The Holy Scriptures teach that:

> "God is not a man, that He should lie, nor a son of man, that He should repent. Has He said, and will He not do? Or has He spoken, and will He not make it good?" (Numbers. 23:19)

So, Yahweh kept His promise to Abraham, Isaac, and Jacob; of which Moses, in testifying about it said:

> "You in Your mercy have led forth the people whom You have redeemed; You have guided them in Your strength to Your holy habitation" (Exodus 15:13)

God is still the Redeemer of Israel even today. Yes, and the Word of the Lord spoken through Isaiah says:

> "But now, thus says the LORD, who created you, O Jacob, And He who formed you, O Israel: "Fear not, for I have redeemed you; I have called *you* by your name; You *are* Mine."
>
> "When you pass through the waters, I *will be* with you; And through the rivers, they shall not overflow you. When you walk through the fire, you shall not be burned, Nor shall the flame scorch you." (Isaiah 43:1-2)

MANKIND'S NEED FOR REDEMPTION

As we have seen with the children of Israel; How Pharaoh dealt shrewdly with them and conspired to enslave them (c.f. Exodus 1), it is also important for us to see that the devil cunningly dealt with Adam and Eve and got the whole world to come under his sway (c.f. Genesis 3). Just as Pharaoh did not conquer the children of Israel through a physical battle, the devil did not also wage physical war against mankind in order to enslave them. He used stealth and deception and played with Man's mind and his undisciplined curiosity because the devil is a liar, a thief, and a crook.

Therefore, every person on earth needs redemption from the oppression and bondage of Satan's kingdom; the kingdom of darkness, which is founded on the principle of *the law of sin and death* (Romans 8:2). The devil had managed to enslave mankind through deception that brought about a diabolic system by which he was able to set in place demonic *taskmasters* to lord it over individuals, families, tribes, communities, cultures, and nations. Through vicious deceit, the devil took advantage over Adam and Eve and thus activated *the law of sin and death* in the earth realm.

When that happened, Man's nature became incompatible with God's glory; sin entered in and he was infected by it. Man, therefore, lost his ability to freely fellowship with God his Creator; he then became afraid and distant from God. Man's relationship with God was then characterized by guilt and shame. We lost our right standing with God and we all became unrighteous. Romans 3:23 says:

> "For all have sinned and fall short of the glory of God."

Thus, the sacrifices of animals without blemish became necessary as a temporal solution for the atonement of Man's sins. The innocent had to die for the guilty in order to compensate for the sins committed. The law of sin and death had been activated and all of humanity came under its power.

With the activation of *the law of sin and death;* curses against Man's welfare were also activated. God had blessed Adam with fruitfulness and prosperity, but now, his relationship with his environment had become characterized by hardship. The ground was cursed, and it was now a toilsome task to earn his living from it. Pain and sorrow were activated and introduced into mankind's experiences.

God said to Eve:

> "I will greatly multiply your sorrow and your conception; in pain, you shall bring forth children; your desire shall be for your husband and he shall rule over you." (Genesis 3:16)

Ungodly desires, depression, slavery and control over fellow mankind, violence, and abuses of all sorts, etc., became the way of life for the peoples of the earth.

In summary, through the devil's stealth and cunning, Mankind came under the *sway* of the evil one, which resulted in the activation of *the law of sin and death* (Romans 8:2). Under the power of the law of sin and death and the sway of the devil, Adam and all after him were subjected to the following:

1. Mankind's relationship with God became broken and access to the tree of life forbidden.
2. Sin and death entered the world, blotting out God's gory that characterized Man at creation.
3. Curses were introduced into the earth realm.
4. Mankind became exposed to hardship for his livelihood.
5. Pain, hurts, cruelties, sickness, disease, and sorrow were introduced into people's lives and experiences.
6. Slavery, murder, strife, violence, selfishness and the abuse of fellow mankind entered the hearts of men.
7. Mankind became vulnerable to all sorts of demonic infestations and harassments.
8. Mankind's eternal destiny was doomed to a Godless eternity in hell.

"Therefore, the son of God was manifested that He might destroy the works of the devil" (1 John 3:8).

THE RANSOM HAS BEEN PAID IN CHRIST

The Bible teaches us in revelation 5:9-10 that Jesus Christ has redeemed us to God by His own blood out of every tribe and tongue and people and nation and has made us kings and priests to our God; and we shall reign on the earth. So, believers should be reigning in life as a normal way of life, which is rightfully theirs to enjoy.

As I stated at the beginning of this chapter, when we discussed redemption in Christ, we are talking about how Christ Jesus, the Son of the Living God, finished His work as our Redeemer to acquire salvation for us through His death and resurrection from the dead.

So, Jesus declared in Mark 10:45, stating that: "… the Son of man did not come to be served, but to serve, and to give His life a ransom for many." As a result, we observe how the Apostle Paul explained it in the first chapter of Ephesians that we are accepted in Christ Jesus the Beloved. And "In Him, we have redemption through His blood."

Therefore, looking at this truth as it applies to the Lord's mission to redeem fallen humanity, the Lord Jesus began His earthly ministry by declaring in Luke 4:18-19 that:

> "The Spirit of the LORD is upon Me, because He has anointed Me to preach the gospel to the poor; He has sent Me to heal the brokenhearted, to proclaim liberty to the captives and recovery of sight to the blind, to set at liberty those who are oppressed; to proclaim the acceptable year of the LORD."

And in Acts 10:38 Peter declared:

> "How God anointed Jesus of Nazareth with the Holy Spirit and with power, who went about doing good and healing

those who were oppressed of the devil, for God was with Him."

John the Baptist had publicly proclaimed Jesus as; "The Lamb of God who takes away the sin of the world!" (John 1:29). Therefore, our Lord Jesus was manifested in the flesh to take away the sin of the World, and that He might destroy the works of the devil. So, because sin had entered the world and death through sin, Jesus Christ laid down His life as our ransom in order to set us free from the law of sin and death. The Bible says:

> "For there is one God and one mediator between God and men, the Man Christ Jesus who gave Himself a ransom for all." (1 Timothy 2:5-6)

My dear friend, I want you to know that: in accordance with the will of our God and Father; the full price for your redemption has been paid by Jesus. You have been redeemed. And this is not just about the redemption from the eternal consequences of your sin, but this also includes the redemption from the powers of this present evil age. This truth is explicitly taught in Paul's letter to the churches in Galatia where he wrote saying:

> "Grace to you and peace from God the Father and our Lord Jesus Christ, who gave Himself for our sins, that he might

deliver us from this present evil age, according to the will of our God and Father" (Galatians 1:3-4).

Jesus Christ has ransomed us from the power of sin, the powers of the devil, and the bondage of sickness and diseases. The Lord Jesus has redeemed all who are His followers from the curse of the law and from all the powers of the kingdom of darkness and has obtained for us eternal redemption. The Bible teaches that God, "…has delivered us from the power of darkness and conveyed us into the kingdom of the Son of His love, in whom we have redemption through His blood, the forgiveness of sins" (Colossians 1:13-14). And so, it is our right to enter the experience of freedom from every form of anguish in our present lives.

JESUS CHRIST HAS REDEEMED US

"But now the righteousness of God apart from the law is revealed, being witnessed by the Law and the Prophets, even the righteousness of God, through faith in Jesus Christ, to all and on all who believe. For there is no difference; for all have sinned and fall short of the glory of God, being justified freely by His grace through the redemption that is in Christ Jesus," (Romans 3:21-24).

"In Him, we have redemption through His blood, the forgiveness of sins, according to the riches of His grace which He made to abound towards us in all prudence" (Ephesians 1:7-8).

"In Him you also trusted, after you heard the word of truth, the gospel of your salvation; in whom also, having believed, you were sealed with the Holy Spirit of promise, who is the guarantee of our inheritance until the redemption of the purchased possession to the praise of His glory" (Ephesians 1:13-14).

BENEFITS OF REDEMPTION

As evident from the Scriptures we can see and should be enjoying the benefits of redemption in Christ which includes the following:

- We have received the gift of God which is eternal life in Christ (Romans 6:23)
- We have received the forgiveness of sins through the blood of Christ (Ephesians. 1:7; Colossians 1:14)
- We have received adoption as sons into God's family through faith in Jesus Christ (Galatians 4:5; Ephesians 1:5).
- We have been redeemed from every lawless deed and wickedness (Titus 2:14).
- We have been delivered from the bondage of sin and the power of the devil (Colossians 1:13).

- We have been delivered from poverty. Jesus became poor so that we through His poverty might become rich (2 Corinthians 8:9).
- By His stripes, we have been healed from all sicknesses and diseases (1 Peter 2:24).
- Christ has redeemed us from the curse of the law having become a curse for us (Galatians 3:13).
- We have peace with God through our Lord Jesus Christ (Romans 5:1)
- In Christ, we have received an abundance of grace and the gift of righteousness (Romans 5:17).
- We have the indwelling of the Holy Spirit within us (1 Corinthians. 6:19-20).
- We have been reconciled to God in Christ (2 Corinthians. 5:18).
- We are seated with Christ in the heavenly places, far above principalities and powers (Ephesians 1:20-21; 2:6).

To be redeemed, then, is to be forgiven of all sin, justified before God's law, be at peace with God, made holy in the sight of God, set free from all bondage to sin and the dominion of darkness; it is to receive abundance of grace and the gift of righteousness, made whole in spirit, soul and body, adopted into God's family, and reconciled to God in Christ.

The word redemption simply means "to recover." The term was used specifically in the Bible in reference to the repurchase or recovery of one's property. The application of this term to Christ's death on the cross is quite revealing. If we are "redeemed," then our prior spiritual condition was one of ownership to another, the devil. God has purchased our freedom through the blood and life of Jesus Christ at Calvary, and we are no longer in bondage to sin or to the kingdom of darkness. And we are no longer in bondage to the law of sin and death. There is therefore now no condemnation for those who are in Christ Jesus, for the law of the Spirit of Life in Christ Jesus has set us free from the law of sin and death (Romans 8:1-2).

Related to the concept of redemption is the word ransom, which describes the price our Lord paid for our release from sin and its consequences. His death was a ransom in exchange for our life. In fact, Scripture is quite clear that redemption in Christ is only possible "through His blood," that is, by His death on the cross and resurrection from the dead (Ephesians. 1:7).

RECKONING YOUR REDEMPTION

Your redemption is a historical fact and It is a reality that is settled in the realms of the spirit. The Lord Jesus has ransomed you from the powers of the dominion of darkness.

This was done over 2000 years ago on the cross of Calvary. The power of sickness and diseases has been broken and you have been redeemed from all curses and all demonic infestations. The full price for your redemption has been paid and you owe the devil nothing that he can claim in your life. On the cross, Jesus declared that it is finished, He paid the full price for your redemption and the devil has been cast out.

But you must understand that the devil is a thief, and his mission is to steal, kill and destroy. Do not let him steal, kill or destroy anything in your life from now on. Submit yourself unto God and resist the devil and he will flee from you. You have been redeemed in Christ and given authority over all the works of the enemy. The one who prowls around, looking for who to devour, is only a toothless bulldog, even when he roars like a lion. He is just the liar, seeking to deceive and destroy the weak, and the careless (1 Peter 5:8-9).

I, therefore, exhort you to get your mind renewed to the reality of these truths and the benefits of your redemption will begin to manifest in your life. Become redemption conscious by meditating day and night on these truths. Give yourself wholeheartedly in the application of these gospel truths in your life. Your daily affirmation of these truths will water your belief and strengthen your faith in Christ. The Bible says:

> For it is with your heart that you believe and are justified, and it is with your mouth that you confess and are saved. (Romans 10:9 NIV)

Your belief in God's word and the confession of your redemption in Christ will locate and position you for the manifestation of your inheritance in Christ. It is in this same fashion that Joshua was commissioned. God commanded him saying:

> "This Book of the Law shall not depart from your mouth, but you shall meditate in it day and night, that you may observe to do according to all that is written in it. For then you will make your way prosperous, and then you will have good success" (Joshua 1:8).

Chapter 6

THE REDEEMING WORK OF CHRIST

The Holy Scriptures reveal that the redeeming work of Christ through the cross was a demonstration of God's love for fallen humanity. At the cross where Christ died for the salvation of all of humanity, God dealt with sin and all unrighteousness, so that anyone who turns to Christ in simple faith might receive forgiveness and be clothed with the righteousness of God in Christ. On the cross, Jesus took upon Himself our sin so that we might be freed from the power of sin and death. He identified Himself with our sin and death so that we might be identified with the Spirit of Life in Christ. He exchanged His life for ours: He was rejected, despised, and became a curse for us so that we might receive His life, be accepted, be blessed and live in the fullness of God's grace.

He laid down His life as a ransom so that we might be redeemed from sin, sickness and diseases, curses, and the power of the devil's dominion. He humbled Himself and became a servant for us to serve us as our Redeemer and High Priest before God.

CHRIST'S INCARNATION

> "And the Word was made flesh, and dwelt among us, (and we beheld his glory, the glory of the only begotten of the Father,) full of grace and truth" (John 1:14).

It was necessary for Jesus to come in the flesh, not just as our Redeemer, but also to manifest the kind of life which we would experience after He had atoned for our sins and redeemed us by His blood.

The Scriptures show us that the fall of Adam opened a door for Satan to sow corruptible seed into the heart of Man. While in the Garden of Eden, Adam submitted to the word of the devil. And the devil's seed of corruption was planted into his life. As a result, his nature and character were then corrupted. So, with Adam being the father of humanity, this corruptible seed was then passed down unto the entire race. Thus, all the descendants of Adam are born with a corruptible nature which is sinful.

But the redeeming work of Christ makes a way for us to receive the blessings of the born-again experience. Attesting to this fact, Watchman Nee (1903–1972) said, "Our old history ends with the cross; our new history begins with the resurrection," in which case we are made partakers of the divine nature through faith in the power of the shed blood of Christ and the finished work of the cross.

The Bible says, "His divine power has given to us all things that pertain to life and godliness, through the knowledge of Him who called us by glory and virtue, by which have been given to us exceedingly great and precious promises, that through these you may be partakers of the divine nature..." (2 Peter 1:3-4).

Just as in Adam, all received Adam's nature of sin which brings death, even so in Christ are we made partakers of the divine nature, through the redemptive power of His precious blood. We have been engrafted into Christ by the operation of the Holy Spirit through *"the word of God, which liveth and abideth for ever."*

All who are born-again are new creations created in Christ to be like God in righteousness and true holiness. The Bible says in Ephesians 4:24 "... *that ye put on the new man, which after God is created in righteousness and true holiness.*" This new man is created after the likeness of the Heavenly Man (1 Corinthians 15:48). Thus, "Our old history ends with the cross; our new history begins with the resurrection." Halleluiah!

THE MYSTERY OF THE GOSPEL

God's plan from the very beginning of time has always been to manifest Himself on the earth through Man. He created Adam and Eve in His image and likeness so as to relate with them as a Father. So, Adam was created a son of God (see Luke 3:38). Adam's nature became poisoned with a false and corruptible seed from the devil the father of lies, and the knowledge of evil was activated in man resulting in the operation of the law of sin and death. Therefore, "For this purpose, the Son of God was manifested, that He might destroy the works of the devil." (1 John 3:8)

The gospel then is about our redemption, reconciliation, restoration of all things and the manifestation of the sons of God on the earth. The devil messed up with the first Adam and took the entire human race captive. Then Jesus came as the Last Adam and paid the ransom for our freedom. The First Man disobeyed in the Garden of Eden, but the Second Man – Jesus, obeyed in the Garden of Gethsemane and at Calvary. The devil defeated the man from the dust, but the Heavenly Man won an eternal victory over the devil and his dominion over Mankind.

For Jesus to do all these wonderful works, He had to put aside His divinity and take on the form of a servant to His Father. He was Perfect Man and a hundred percent Divine in His nature. But as the Last Adam with a mission to recover what the First Adam had lost; Jesus had to face the Will of the Father in the Garden of Gethsemane. He did it as a Man so that He may terminate with the Adamic sin on that Cross of Calvary.

In Eden, Adam disobeyed God, so Jesus had to reverse that disobedience in Gethsemane through His obedience to God. He accomplished this by submitting His will to the will of the Father and by accepting to lay down His life through the death of the cross. He could only do this to redeem us as a Perfect Man, He had to be without sin. Sin was what caused the devil to be kicked out of Heaven, and sin was the cause of Man's Fall and enslavement by the evil one, the devil. So, Jesus could not use His divinity in the process. I believe that this was the reason why His agony was so intense that His sweat was like great drops of blood (see Luke 22:44). It was a fierce battle that required a great sacrifice that only divine providence could supply. As the last Adam, representing humanity, human ego was being dismantled and the corruptible seed of evil which was sown in Eden was destroyed.

In my opinion, all servants of God must experience a personal Gethsemane in order to be worthy of that appellation. Absolute surrender to the will of God as modeled by Jesus is essential to experiencing the victorious life in Christ. I believe this to be the key to the manifestation of Christ's life in and through us.

HE WAS REJECTED

Jesus paid a heavy price on His way to and at Calvary, for our restoration to God. He was rejected and despised by men. The prophet Isaiah prophesied about this and said:

> "He is despised and rejected by men. A man of sorrows and acquainted with grief. And we hid, as it were, our faces from Him; He was despised, and we did not esteem Him" (Isaiah 53:3).

You know, rejection is the feeling of being despised, unwelcomed, un-esteemed, undesired and unwanted. This spirit of rejection came about after Adam sinned. For, every sin is an offense towards God which estranges the sinner from God. So, Jesus took upon Himself to ransom mankind from the spiritual stronghold of rejection caused by sin and thus made us acceptable in and through the Beloved Son of God.

Jesus went through rejection for you and me as He was rejected by the chief priest, the elders and the people of Israel, who handed Him as a state criminal to Pilate. They requested the release of a hardened criminal called Barabbas in His place and demanded that He be crucified. The Roman soldiers also mocked, despised and rejected Jesus who was the Savior of all Mankind. They spat on Him, pulled his beard and struck Him on the head. He was also scourged and humiliated; He was bruised for our iniquities and by His stripes, we were healed (Isaiah 53:4). And He went through all of these for our sake and our redemption.

My dear friend, know that you who are in Christ have been accepted by God the Father and the spirit of rejection has been broken over your life. When Jesus cried out on the cross "My God, My God, why have you forsaken Me?" He was bearing upon Himself all the sins of Humanity and receiving the righteous judgment of God which made Him feel abandoned and forsaken. He was forsaken because of our sin; so that you and I could be forgiven and accepted. That is why He says, *"I will never leave you nor forsake you"* (Hebrews 13:5). The full price has been paid. Let no man cheat you through philosophy or the traditions of men. If God is for you, who can be against you; and if God has justified you, who can condemn you? God has accepted you, my dear friend in Christ, no one can reject you. So, enter and experience and enjoy the blessings of your redemption in the risen Christ. Hallelujah!

HE WAS CRUCIFIED

At the cross, the sin problem of man was settled through the blood of His crucifixion. Through His shed blood at the cross, Jesus atoned for our sins and reconciled us to God. He not only shed His blood for our sins, but He died in our place so that we might be delivered from the nature and power of sin. Our old man was crucified with Him that the power of sin might be destroyed.

> Knowing this, that our old man is crucified with him, that the body of sin might be destroyed, and henceforth we should not serve sin. For he that is dead is freed from sin. Now if we are dead with Christ, we believe that we shall also live with him. (Romans 6:6-8)

The knowledge of the fact that our old-man, or the original sin nature received from Adam, was crucified with Christ is very important as the first step for anyone seeking to enter and experience freedom from sin. My dear friend, do you know that your "old-man" was crucified with Christ? If yes then, pray that these facts may become "divine" revelation in your heart and life, and I guarantee that your life will be transformed for the better and the best. I know this for a fact, and I enjoy the experience. For, I remember very vividly when this blessed experience was bestowed in my heart. It was like a butterfly's experience when it breaks out of its cocoon. The power of sin in me was broken, and I felt empowered in my inner-man. What a blessed experience! I believe that this is what the old-timers called "The Blessing of Sanctification." (Hebrews 10:14)

We are not only to have this knowledge (knowledge of the fact that we have been crucified with Christ), but we must likewise reckon ourselves in the light of redemption to be dead indeed to sin with Christ.

> "For in that he died, he died unto sin once: but in that he liveth, he liveth unto God. Likewise reckon ye also yourselves to be dead indeed unto sin, but alive unto God through Jesus Christ our Lord" (Romans 6:10-11).

Yes, a reckoning is the next very important step in maintaining your freedom from sin after you have received the revelation of knowing that: "He that is dead is freed from sin." Reckoning is like keeping records of financial transactions. So, likewise, you also reckon yourself to be dead indeed unto sin, but alive unto God. This will serve you to fight the good fight of faith when the enemy comes with temptations of doubt and unbelief after the emotions of your "knowing" experience have subsided. Always remember that:

> The Blood deals with what we have done, whereas the Cross deals with what we are. The Blood disposes of our

sins, while the Cross strikes at the root of our capacity for sin. (Watchman Nee, *The Normal Christian Life*)

"But if we walk in the light, as he is in the light, we have fellowship with one another, and the blood of Jesus, his Son, purifies us from every sin." (1 John 1:7)

On the cross, Jesus settled the issue of guilt and condemnation, and all unrighteousness through the washing by His blood. Hence, reconciling us to God and giving us right standing with the Father in Christ. That is why the Bible says: *"If we confess our sins, he is faithful and just and will forgive us our sins and purify us from all unrighteousness" (1 John 1:9).*

Hebrews 9:14 says, *"How much more shall the blood of Christ, who through the eternal Spirit offered himself without spot to God, purge your conscience from dead works to serve the living God?"*

HE WAS BURIED

When Christ was buried, he descended into the lower parts of the earth, and defeated Satan, destroyed his works over man and stripped him of all his powers. You know, sin was the means through which Satan held mankind in captivity. So, when the Lord Jesus Christ died on the cross, He was crucified as the last Adam. All that happened with the first Adam was summed-up in His sacrificial death and was done away with on the cross. As the last Adam, Jesus destroyed sin and all the powers of darkness with it.

"For this purpose, the Son of God was manifested, that he might destroy the works of the devil." (1 John 3:8)

And in Colossian 2:15 the Bible says,

"And having spoiled principalities and powers, he made a shew of them openly, triumphing over them in it."

Through His death and burial, Jesus ruined Satan and his works as it relates to us who are in Christ. Therefore, Satan has no power whatsoever over anyone that is in Christ. My dear brothers and sisters, Satan has no authority over your life. He was stripped of all his authority and all his claims of accusations against the sons of God. Jesus said in John 12:31: "Now is the judgment of this world; now the ruler of this world will be cast out." Amen. This is now a done deal and not something to take place in the future. The work has been done. It is finished!

"Then I heard a loud voice saying in heaven, "Now salvation, and strength, and the kingdom of our God, and the power of His Christ have come, for the accuser of our brethren, who accused them before our God day and night, has been cast down. And they overcame him by the blood of the Lamb and by the word of their testimony, and they did not love their lives to the death." (Revelation 12:10-11)

The precious blood of Christ is the means by which all who are in Christ are redeemed, and it is in virtue of the efficacy of the atonement that we are enabled to be victorious over the powers of the devil. You and I are victors in Christ. For, greater is He who is in us than he who is in the world.

HE WAS RAISED FROM THE DEAD

I believe that the resurrection of Christ from the dead was the demonstration of the victory over the power of the corruptible seed that was sown into the soul of mankind, and the dead works with which it held mankind in captivity.

> "This is why it says: 'When he ascended on high, he led captives in his train and gave gifts to men.'" (Ephesians 4:8)

Jesus destroyed the power of death and defied its claims by His resurrection – *"O death, where is thy sting? O grave, where is thy victory?" (1 Corinthians 15:55)*, – thus translating us from the kingdom of darkness into the kingdom of His marvelous light. We, therefore, rejoice in Christ, "Knowing that Christ being raised from the dead dies no more: death has no more dominion over him" (Romans 6:9). The Bible further teaches that:

> "For he has rescued us from the dominion of darkness and brought us into the kingdom of the Son he loves," (Colossians 1:13).

We who are in Christ are partakers in all that He went through on the cross, including His victory over death and over the kingdom of darkness. His resurrection was for our deliverance from the law of sin and death-- our freedom from sin and all its bondages-- our sanctification, and our restoration and reconciliation to God the Father. When He arose from the dead, He activated and set in motion the law of the Spirit of life in Christ Jesus. This is why Paul the Apostle says:

> "There is therefore now no condemnation to those who are in Christ Jesus, who do not walk according to the flesh, but according to the Spirit. For the law of the Spirit of life in Christ Jesus has made me free from the law of sin and death." (Romans 8:1-2)

HE ASCENDED AND IS SEATED

The Lord Jesus Christ, after satisfying the condition for our redemption and making us acceptable to the Father who adopted us as sons of God and joint-heirs with Him, ascended and sat at the right hand of God the Father in Majesty.

> "Far above principality and power, and might, and dominion and every name that is named, and not only in this world but also in that which is to come: and has put all things under his feet, and gave him to be the head over all things to the church." (Ephesians 1:21-22)

> "… And hath raised us up together and made us sit together in the heavenly places in Christ Jesus." (Ephesians 2:6)

We are seated with Christ at the right hand of God the Father. Our position in Christ is elevated; far above principalities and powers and might and dominion and every name that is named and not only in this world but also in that which is to come. Hallelujah!

Seated with Christ, we have been given a position of authority and we are reigning with Him in the heavenly places. This, I believe, is the revelation of the kingdom of God amongst men; in that Christ completed His work of redemption by restoring the dominion position of mankind on the earth and right standing with the Father, making us a royal priesthood to represent our God and also to reign in the earth. This is in perfect harmony with what the Bible teaches, where it states:

> "But you are a chosen people, a royal priesthood, a holy nation, a people belonging to God, that you may declare the praises of him who called you out of darkness into his wonderful light." (1 Peter 2:9)

The born-again experience brings with it the restoration of all that Adam lost in the Garden of Eden. That is, the born-again believer is recreated in Christ and given the same position of authority, Adam had before the fall and much more, even the dominion over the works of the devil in setting men free from the devil's oppression.

> "Then God blessed them, and God said to them, Be fruitful and multiply; fill the earth and subdue it; have dominion over the fish of the sea, over the birds of the air, and over every living thing that moves on the earth." (Genesis 1:28)

TAKE TIME AND PRAISE GOD

Now then, take some time and worship the Lord for His immense love and sacrifice on the cross and for the redemption that was wrought on our behalf. He has redeemed us completely and restored us to the dominion position over the earth. We are not just saved from our sins or the consequences and power of sin, but He has crowned us with glory and honor for heavenly citizenship and granted us access to the resources of heaven.

I thank You, Lord, for the blessings of Calvary.

In Psalms 107:8,9 the Psalmist says:

> "Oh, that men would praise the LORD for his goodness, and for his wonderful works to the children of men! For, He

satisfieth the longing soul, and filleth the hungry soul with goodness."

And in verses 15 and 16 he again says:

"Oh, that men would praise the LORD for his goodness, and for his wonderful works to the children of men! For he hath broken the gates of brass and cut the bars of iron in sunder."

A WORD OF PRAYER

I thank You, Lord Jesus, for the cross where you died for my salvation. Yes Lord, Oh! With all my heart, I thank You Lord for paying the full price to redeem me. You have brought me out of darkness into light, out of the shadows of death to the comforts of life, even that abundant life which is in Christ. I was bound but You have set me free and made me free from within my innermost being. You broke the chains that held me bound asunder and used them on my foe. Lord Jesus, You cut and opened wide the prison doors so that I could walk out in freedom without fear and You took captivity captive. I rejoice in Your victory, the victory of the Cross.

Oh, freedom is mine. For, "If the Son, therefore, shall make you free, ye shall be free indeed." (John 8:36) Amen

Chapter 7

RECONCILIATION IN CHRIST

Imagine a child that was exposed to, and infected by a deadly virus; all because of his own negligence, and disobedience to the parents' instructions and strict warnings. So, because of this viral infection, the child's DNA was altered, and as a result, the child could no longer live with the parents. The parents' living environment had become very uncomfortable for the child's now altered nature. It was then necessary for the child to be separated from the parents' home forever. The good relationship they once enjoyed was broken, and the child's relationship with the parents is now characterized by guilt and shame.

Such estrangement could only be reversed by the means of an antidote against the viral infection that was capable of bringing about the restoration of the child's damaged DNA. So, in the course of time, an antidote was eventually discovered and prepared for the rescue of the child's life. When the antidote was applied against the deadly virus, the child's life was rescued, which resulted in the restoration of the damaged DNA. After the child was cured and made whole, reconciliation between the parents and the child was then possible.

Oh, what a joy it was on that day when it finally happened. The child was now at home with his parents. The antidote had dealt with the poisonous nature of the deadly virus: breaking its destructive power, healing and restoring the altered nature of the child.

This child was restored and reconciled to the parents and that was a wonderful thing. But during the long estrangement of this child from the parents, the child had acquired habits and behaviors which were consistent with life under the deadly viral infection. Now that reconciliation has taken place, there is a need for the child to abandon those old habits and behaviors and to relearn the habits and behaviors that are consistent with his new life in the parent's environment and culture.

The picture I have just painted above is an illustration of humanity's lost condition in sin without God and of what

Jesus' blood has accomplished for our salvation through His sacrificial death on the cross of Calvary.

ALL THINGS BECOME NEW IN CHRIST

To be reconciled is simply to be restored to fellowship and harmony. When old friends resolve their differences and restore their relationship, reconciliation has occurred. The Bible says;

> If anyone is in Christ, he is a new creation, old things have passed away, behold all things have become new. (2 cor. 5:17)

The key phrase here is "if anyone is in Christ." For, there are people who are not yet in Christ. If anyone is not in Christ, he is obviously an old creation and he cannot possibly experience reconciliation with God. Those who are in Christ are no more under any condemnation from God because they have been redeemed. The law of the Spirit of life in Christ Jesus has set them free from the law of sin and death. They have become a new creation and old things have passed away. The blood of Christ is to them God's antidote to the sin problem that infected humanity and corrupted the spiritual DNA of all men. The blood of Jesus, in this case, deals directly with the destructive nature of sin and its poisonous effects on the human spirit. In Revelation 1:5-6 John the revelator proclaimed this truth in saying:

> "To him who loves us and has freed us from our sins by his own blood, and has made us be a kingdom of priests to serve his God and Father" – (NIV)

This truth is further revealed in Romans 5:9-11 where the Bible says,

> "Since we have now been justified by his blood, how much more shall we be saved from God's wrath through him! For if, when we were God's enemies, we were reconciled to him through the death of his Son, how much more, having been reconciled, shall we be saved through his life! Not only is this so, but we also rejoice in God through our Lord Jesus Christ, through whom we have now received reconciliation" – (NIV)

The fact that we needed reconciliation reveals that our relationship with God was broken. We were separated from God because of sin. Our sin alienated us from Him, rendering us incompatible with His glory.

> "For, all have sinned and fall short of the glory of God." (Romans 3:23)

When Christ died on the cross, He satisfied God's righteous judgment on sin and made it possible for us to be at peace with Him. Our "reconciliation" to God then, did not only, involve the exercise of His grace and the forgiveness of our sin, but it is also that the blood of Jesus washed us from the stain of sin. Reconciliation in Christ is a glorious truth that demonstrates the effectiveness of the blood of Christ to redeem mankind from his fallen state.

We were by nature separated from God and heading towards perdition but are now through the blood of Christ His children who have received eternal life. We were in a state of condemnation because of our sins, but we are now justified and brought near. We were by nature at war with God, but now we have the peace that transcends all understanding (Philippians 4:7).

GOD THE AUTHOR OF RECONCILIATION

In 2 Corinthians 5:18 the Bible teaches that every change that has taken place in our spirits was God's doing.

> "Now all things are of God, who has reconciled us to Himself through Jesus Christ."

And there is no sin or corruption in the born-again spirit. The problem that caused separation between God and man was sin. God took the initiative to remove this barrier through the means and agency of Jesus Christ, thus leaving God and man as friends once again.

"In justification, there is the picture of the criminal before his judge, with the judge pronouncing a sentence of acquittal; so, in reconciliation, there is the picture of the once-estranged child before his father, with the alienation now replaced by peace. God due to his constant love, takes the initiative, breaks into man's hostility, and throws down every barrier to an enduring and marvelous relationship. God takes the initiative; man, merely responds. God is the subject of reconciliation; man is the object of reconciliation. God does the reconciling, and man is the one who is reconciled; it is the latter whose attitude is basically changed" (Doctrines of the Christian Religion by William W. Stevens [DOTCR], pp.239-241).

THE MINISTRY OF RECONCILIATION IN CHRIST

It is important to realize that we have been entrusted with the ministry of reconciliation. That means that we are in the ministry of reconciling people to God.

"Now all things are of God, who has reconciled us to Himself through Jesus Christ, and has given us the ministry of reconciliation, that is, that God was in Christ reconciling the world to Himself, not imputing their trespasses to them, and he has committed to us the word of reconciliation. We are therefore Christ's ambassadors, as though God were making his appeal through us. We implore you on Christ's behalf: Be reconciled to God." (2 Cor. 5:18-20 NIV)

RENEW YOUR MIND

"Once you were alienated from God and were enemies in your minds because of your evil behavior". (Col. 1:21 NIV)

The alienation and the enmity that exists between man and God is seated in our minds and therefore manifests itself through our evil behavior. It is not God who rejected us. We rejected God by exalting our own wisdom above the wisdom of God. Therefore, since our minds were what led us away from God, the renewing of our minds must be part of the process of restoring us back to God

At salvation, it is our spirit which is "born-again." Note that our mind is not instantly changed. In fact, we must make our thinking change by believing the truths of God's Word. Since the alienation was in our minds, then we will continue to experience alienation, even after we are "born-again," until our thinking changes. Understand that this reconciliation was accomplished through the death of our Lord Jesus (Colossians 1:22). The awful price that was paid indicates the greatness of the debt. This harmony was not cheap and should never be taken lightly. Jesus paid an indescribably awful price for our reconciliation. He was subjected to sorrow and humiliation; he was rejected by men and despised. He died in my place and for my reconciliation.

THE FATHER'S HOUSE

> "Let not your heart be troubled; you believe in God, believe also in Me. In My Father's house are many mansions; if it were not so, I would have told you. I go to prepare a place for you. And if I go and prepare a place for you, I will come again and receive you to Myself; that where I am, there you may be also." (John 14:1-4)

Jesus came to reconcile us to the Father. God is our Father, but we only become His children after we are born-again. You see, children are either born into a family or they are adopted. But we have both experiences in Christ. We're born-again children as well as adopted children of God. You may be asking yourself and wondering about the difference between becoming a child of God by adoption and the new birth.

Well in Ephesians 1:4-5 the Bible says:

"According as he hath chosen us in him before the foundation of the world, that we should be holy and without blame before him in love: Having predestinated us unto the adoption of children by Jesus Christ to himself, according to the good pleasure of his will."

And 2 Thessalonians 2:13-14 also says:

"But we are bound to give thanks to God always for you, brethren beloved by the Lord, because God from the beginning chose you for salvation through sanctification by the Spirit and belief in the truth, to which he called you by our gospel, for the obtaining of the glory of our Lord Jesus Christ."

You see, God made a decisive choice to adopt you as His child through Christ Jesus in accordance with His good pleasure. This was in relation to your history during which you were by nature a child of the devil; you were separated from God and heading towards perdition. He made this choice before you ever accepted Jesus as your Lord and Savior, but this adoption experience only became a reality in your life the day that you received Christ and believed in the name of Jesus.

The moment you placed your faith for salvation based on the merits of Christ and received forgiveness for your sins, the Holy Spirit did an operation that recreated your spirit. You were born-again and joint with Christ as one and reconciliation with the Father also took place.

Adoption then is in relation to our history before Christ in that God purposed to make us His children and the new birth is in relation to the divine act of our spirit-man being made anew, created in true righteousness and holiness after the image of God. We were adopted and reborn at the same instant that we accepted and acknowledged Jesus as our personal Savior. What a mystery.

Therefore, as God's children, there is a place in the

Father's house for each one of us. We have an inheritance prepared for us by Jesus in the Father's house. This is not just a promise for life in eternity as it is traditionally believed, but it is a place into the very presence of God.

We had lost our place in the Father's house. We were estranged from the Father because of sin, and the sin nature in man needed to be dealt with. And Jesus was manifested to deal with this problem. Therefore, He had to go to the Father's house after His resurrection to prepare a place for us, so that we can be at home with Him again as dear children of God. Jesus came as our Redeemer, to redeem us from sin and death, and to reconcile us as beloved children unto the Father.

Chapter 8

IDENTITY IN CHRIST

"When Jesus came into the region of Caesarea Philippi, He asked his disciples, saying, "Who do men say that I, the Son of Man, am?"

So, they said, "Some say John the Baptist, some Elijah, and others Jeremiah or one of the prophets."

He said to them, "But what do you say that I am?"

Simon Peter answered and said, "You are the Christ, the Son of the Living God."

Jesus answered and said to him, "Blessed are you, Simon Bar-Jonah, for flesh and blood has not revealed this to you, but My Father who is in heaven. And I also say to you that you are Peter, and on this rock, I will build my church, and the gates of hades shall not prevail against it. And I will

Identity in Christ

> give you the keys of the kingdom of heaven, and whatever you bind on earth will be bound in heaven, and whatever you loose on earth will be loosed in heaven." (Matthew 16:13-19)

In these passages of Scripture, Jesus asked His disciples two very important questions: *"Who do men say that I, the Son of Man, am?"* and *"Who do you say that I am?"* The first question Jesus asked was on the confession of men about His identity. It is worth noting that Jesus was interested to know what the disciples had heard or learned from what people were saying about His identity. When they answered and said:

> Some say John the Baptist, some Elijah, and others Jeremiah or one of the prophets (Matthew 16:14).

Jesus did not tell the disciples to discard what was being said by outsiders. But after listening to what men said, He the Son of Man was, He asked them about their own personal confession of His identity. *"Who do you say that I am?*

> Simon Peter answered and said, "You are the Christ, the Son of the Living God." (Matthew 16:16)

WHO IS JESUS TO YOU?

Is your knowledge of Jesus based only on what others have said? Who is Jesus to you? Do you know Him in a personal way? Many professing Christians do not have a personal revelation of who Jesus is. If they have any revelation at all, it is flesh and blood-based, which is often void of the power that comes with divine revelation. When Peter said,

> "You are the Christ, the Son of the Living God,"
>
> Jesus answered and said to him, "Blessed are you, Simon Bar-Jonah, for flesh and blood has not revealed this to you, but My Father who is in heaven." (Matt 16:17)

Jesus' true identity as the Christ, the Son of the Living God must be received by divine revelation from God the Father. This is clearly taught in John 6:44-45 where Jesus declared that:

> "No one can come to Me unless the Father who sent Me draws him… It is written in the prophets, *"And they shall all be taught by God"* Therefore anyone who has heard and learned from the Father comes to Me."

Somebody may be reading this and be mightily blessed. Yes, and truly so, but if It is not received as divine revelation from the Father, and if the voice of God's Spirit is not heeded and learned from, the divine revelation that reveals Christ to men will not be imparted into his spirit. Such a person would have received revelation at the level of flesh and blood. And flesh and blood revelation always fall short of getting the individual into the revelation of his identity in Christ. This is because spiritual truths are only revealed to us through the workings of the Holy Spirit.

> "The man without the Spirit does not accept the things that come from the Spirit of God, for they are foolishness to him, and he cannot understand them, because they are spiritually discerned." (1 Cor. 2:14 NIV)

DIVINE REVELATION OF THE BELIEVER'S IDENTITY IN CHRIST

After Peter had confessed Jesus as the Christ, the Son of the Living God, Jesus blessed him and confirmed that the Father was the source of Peter's revelation. In Matthew 16:18, the Lord Jesus now begins to reveal to Peter his new identity in Christ. God the Father had revealed Christ to Peter, and Christ was, in turn, revealing to Peter who he has become in Christ after God the Father had granted to him (Peter) a revelation of who Jesus was. So, Jesus said:

> "And I also say to you that you are Peter, and on this rock, I will build My church, and the gates of Hades shall not prevail against it." (Matthew 16:18)

In a sense, I could imagine that Jesus was declaring to Simon Peter something similar to this:

> *"Peter, because of this revelation from the Father to you about Me; you have heard and learned from the Father what My true identity is. I now reveal to you who you have become in Me. You are Petros, which means a piece of rock that is a part of the massive rock, Petra, which I am. See Peter, you and I are now of the same spiritual nature and substance. This revelation that you received from the Father about My identity has been used by the Holy Spirit to cause you to be joined to Me and thus made you and I one spirit. For he who is joined to the Lord is one spirit with Him (1 Corinthians 6:17). That is the kind of revelation I will build my church on, and the gates of hades shall not prevail against it."* (Author's paraphrase)

The Greek word translated "Peter" in Matthew 16:18 is *Petros (Strong's #4074)*, while the Greek word translated "rock" is *Petra (Strong's #4073)*. *Petros* is a piece of *Petra*; so also, are all believers who are in Christ. All who put their trust in Jesus for salvation, are members of His body. They come "to Him as to a living stone." And they "also as living stones are being built up as a spiritual house, a holy priesthood, to offer up spiritual sacrifices acceptable to God through Jesus Christ (1 Peter 2:4-5). The believer in Christ is a member/part of Christ in his spirit-man. Thus, the church of Christ is built on this revelation. "Now you are the body of

Identity in Christ

Christ, and members individually" (1 Corinthians. 12:27). Christ and His church are one, just as the head and the body of any individual are one. Christ is the Head of the Church which is His Body. That was why Jesus rebuked Saul of Tarsus on his way to Damascus as he persecuted the early Church.

> "Saul, Saul, why are you persecuting Me?"
>
> And he said, "Who are you, Lord?"
>
> Then the Lord said, "I am Jesus whom you are persecuting" (Acts 9:4-5)

Saul had never persecuted the physical flesh and blood Jesus, but because he was persecuting followers of Jesus, the Lord took it as Saul persecuting Him. This is because all who are in Christ Jesus are one spirit with Him. Yes, you are one spirit with Christ, you have been washed by the precious blood of Christ and are born-again by the Spirit of God.

> "But he who unites himself with the Lord is one with him in spirit." (1 Corinthians 6:17 NIV)

BAPTIZED INTO THE BODY OF CHRIST

> "For by one Spirit we were all baptized into one body– whether Jews or Greeks, slave or free– and have all been made to drink into one Spirit." (1 Cor. 12:13)

Baptism into the body of Christ is the same as being "born-again". When we are born-again, the Holy Spirit places us into the body of Christ. We become a part of God's family with God as our Eternal Father. This baptism takes place spiritually when we receive Jesus as the Christ, the Son of the living God, putting our faith in Him for salvation, and making Him Lord over our lives. In 1 Corinthians 6:17 the bible teaches that: "He who is joined to the Lord is one spirit with Him" Therefore, there is a new spiritual nature imparted in us. The nature of God has been implanted within us when Jesus came into our lives as Lord and Savior. We are now a new creation and sons of the living God. Thus, the Bible says:

> Therefore, if anyone is in Christ, he is a new creation; old things have passed away; behold, all things have become new. (2 Cor. 5:17)

> But as many as received Him, to them He gave the right to become children of God, to those who believe in His name. (John 1:12)

A NEW MAN IN CHRIST

You who are born-again have become a new man in Christ. The liberating truth about this is that, in Christ you have received divine ability and the responsibility to "...put off, concerning your former conduct, the old man which grows corrupt according to the deceitful lusts, and *be renewed in the spirit of your mind,* and that you put on the new man which was created according to God, in true righteousness and holiness." (Ephesians 4:22-24)

Your spirit-man in Christ has been created in true righteousness and holiness like God's. So, it can be rightly said that the born-again child of God has been recreated in the image and likeness of God, that is, in true righteousness and holiness. When you asked Jesus to come into your life and save you, God sent forth the Spirit of His Son into your heart. Thus, the Bible goes on to say:

> And because you are sons, God sent forth the Spirit of His Son into your hearts, crying out "Abba, Father!" (Galatians. 4:6).

There is a newness of life that has been imparted into your spirit-man and that is what made you a son of God. This new life can be manifested through you if you reckon its source and renew your mind to conform to your real identity in Christ.

Let me recall to your attention that in chapters 5 and 6 of this book, we have discussed in detail how Christ has redeemed us completely from the consequences of the Fall. Now then, with the understanding of these truths, and the fact that we have been baptized into Christ, therefore, Romans 6:4 teaches that "…just as Christ was raised from the dead by the glory of the Father, even so, we also should walk in the newness of life." This newness of life is a life in the glory of the Father; a life in which *"your kingdom come; your will be done on earth as it is heaven"* can be your everyday experience. This is a mystery and that, "...God willed to make known what the riches of the glory of this mystery among the Gentiles are: which is Christ in you the hope of glory" (Colossians 1:27).

THE FULLNESS OF CHRIST IN YOU

The fullness of Christ has been deposited in your spirit by the Holy Spirit. The Scriptures declare in John 1:16 that: "And of His fullness, we have all received." If you believe this Scripture, which I think you do if you have confessed Jesus as your Savior, you should also understand that you have equally received all the fullness of God in Christ. Note that the word received in John 1:16 is in the past tense. God's fullness in Christ is already in your possession. You've already got it and it is a spiritual reality. This is a truth that is reiterated in many other Scriptures.

> For God was pleased to have all his fullness dwell in him. (Colossians 1:19 NIV)

And you have received that fullness when you received Christ Jesus as Lord and Savior over your life. You

Identity in Christ

can now function on the earth with the same authority and power that Jesus operated in while He walked the face of the earth.

This may sound too good to be true, yet It is the good news of the gospel. You can do all things through Christ who strengthens you from within. For, it is all by His grace, His anointing, His authority and His power that you have been given this fullness and glory.

> See to it that no one takes you captive through hollow and deceptive philosophy, which depends on human tradition and the basic principles of this world rather than on Christ.
>
> For in Christ all the fullness of the Deity lives in bodily form, and you have been given fullness in Christ, who is the head over every power and authority. (Colossians 2:8-10 NIV)

This fullness of Christ that we have received is not automatically manifested into our daily experience. Even though God's divine power dwells within our spirit-man in all its totality; we may live all our lives as Christians and die like mere men, without benefiting from the blessings that God's divine power has made available to us. This is because the manifestation of this power in our life is in accordance with how it is at work within us. Ephesians 3:20 says:

Now to Him who is able to do exceedingly abundantly above all that we ask or think, according to the power that works in us.

In 2 Peter 1:3, we are told that "...His divine power has given to us all things that pertain to life and godliness, through the knowledge of Him who called us by glory and virtue." You see, there is nothing lacking and nothing missing in God's provision for His children to successfully live the abundant life. It is according to the power that is at work within us. If little power is at work within us, certainly, little power will be manifested through us. Quite simply, isn't it?

"But we have this treasure in earthen vessels, that the excellence of the power may be of God and not us." (2 Corinthians 4:7)

ADVENTURES WITH GOD

Dearly beloved, you and I are called into a wonderful life of adventures with God. Knowing who we are in Christ and being able to release the power within our spirit man is the gateway to the real life of adventures with God. I believe that the following testimony which is an excerpt from John G. Lake's book: *Adventures in God,* will stir you up for personal adventures with God.

Identity in Christ

"One evening in my own tabernacle, a young girl about 16 to 18 years of age by the name of Hilda suddenly became overpowered by the Spirit of God. She arose and stood on the platform beside me. I recognized at once that the Lord had given the girl a message, so I simply stopped preaching and waited while the Spirit of God came upon her. She began to chant in some language I did not know, and then made gestures like those a Mohammedan priest would make when chanting prayers. In the back of the house, I observed a young East Indian, whom I knew. He became enraptured and commenced to walk gradually up the aisle. No one disturbed him, and he proceeded up the aisle until he had reached the front. Then he stood looking into the girl's face with intense amazement. When her message had ceased, I said to him, "What is it?" He answered, "Oh, she speaks my language!" I said, "What does she say?" He came upon the platform beside me and gave the gist of her message. "She tells me that salvation comes from God. In order to save men, Jesus Christ, Who was God, became a man. She says one man cannot save another; that Mohammed was a man like other men, not a "power" to save a man from his sins. But Jesus was God, and He had the power to impart His Spirit to me and make me like God."

Chapter 9

THE AUTHORITY OF THE BELIEVER

"And I will give you the keys of the kingdom of heaven, and whatever you bind on earth will be bound in heaven, and whatever you loose on earth will be loosed in heaven". (Matt. 16:19)

In this chapter I want us to look into the authority which God has given to us as believers. I believe that in order to address this effectively, we have to deal not only with the authority we have in Christ but also the authority of Satan. Many Christians have been led to believe that they are fighting an adversary whose power is superior to theirs and are thus just barely able to cope with him. The truth though, is that Satan is an influence; he does exist, and he has a hierarchy of principalities and powers that we are fighting against, but he is a defeated and disarmed foe. So, the Bible teaches that we should:

> "Put on the whole armor of God, that you may be able to stand against the wiles of the devil" (Ephesians 6:11-12).

The power that Satan really has against believers is deception. He doesn't have the power to just overcome anyone at will. As I have mentioned in chapter 5 of this book, under the section on *Man's need for Redemption*, it is important for us to see that the devil cunningly dealt with Adam and Eve to deceive them to fall into sin and, through sin, he got the whole world to come under his sway. He did not conquer Adam and Eve through a physical battle, and neither did he use some spiritual powers to fight against them. He used stealth and deception and played with Eve's mind and tricked her undisciplined curiosity.

In Genesis 3 we see that when the devil came against Adam and Eve, he did not use some superior force, but he inhabited a snake, which was the most subtle creature that God had made. The word "subtle" means "sly, deceptive, or cunning." The reason Satan came through the snake was that he really did not have the power to force Adam and Eve to do anything against their will. He could not even intimidate them. So, he resorted to deception. And that is how he has operated ever since.

Now, concerning the authority of the believer, you have to recognize that Satan has zero power and authority over you in Christ. You have been redeemed from his domain and translated into the Kingdom of God's beloved Son. Satan is a defeated and disarmed foe. The only way he can gain power against you is to come at you with lies, deceptions, enticements, seductions, and temptations in an effort to get you to sin against God.

In 2 Corinthians 10:3-5 the Bible says,

> "For though we walk in the flesh, we do not war after the flesh: (For the weapons of our warfare are not carnal, but mighty through God to the pulling down of strongholds;) Casting down imaginations, and every high thing that exalts itself against the knowledge of God, and bringing into captivity every thought to the obedience of Christ."

Notice that these scriptures are talking about the weapons of our warfare which are not carnal, "we do not war according to the flesh," and every weapon that is mentioned in this passage refers to our mind, dealing with our thoughts. It is important for you to understand that Satan does not have the power to do anything to you except through your thoughts and with the aim to deceive and enslave you.

GOD, THE SOURCE OF ALL AUTHORITY

God is the source of all authority that exists. Yes! That is rightly so, for, in the beginning, God had all authority. All power and authority have to come from God because He is the only one who has power in Himself. Everything else is delegated from Him. When God created the heavens and the earth, He had all power and authority. Then in Genesis 1:26, when God created Adam and Eve, He said, *"Let them have dominion…over all the earth."* And we also see in Psalm 115:16, that, *"The heaven, even the heavens, are the LORD'S: but the earth hath he given to the children of men."* So, God had ownership of everything by right of being the Creator, but He gave dominion, or authority, over the earth to physical human beings. Satan has never had the legitimate right and power to rule over the earth. He got it through deception. God gave power to mankind, and when they fell, they yielded their God-given authority and power over to the devil. So, Satan was never given power by God to oppress mankind or to have the right to rule this earth. It is true that the Bible does say that Satan is the god of this world, but it is not because God made him the god of this world. He became the god of this world by deceiving mankind into signing away their God-given power and authority over to him. God never put Satan in a position above mankind. He gave mankind dominion and authority over this earth.

The only reason Satan has ever been able to oppress, dominate, or cause the problems he does, is that Adam and Eve yielded their God-given authority to him. This created a real problem for God. It was a problem to God, because God was a Spirit, and He had given authority over this earth to physical human beings. Only people who had a physical body were given the authority and power to rule and exercise influence on this earth. That was the reason, Satan had to come to Eve and got her to yield their authority to him. That is the reason why Satan's activities on earth must involve the use of a human body. In Scriptures, demons had to have a body to possess in order for them to exercise their influence on the earth. This is because Satan cannot do anything unless he is using a physical human body to work through.

Now, because God was a Spirit and He had given authority to physical human beings, so in a sense, He had a limitation placed on Himself as far as His intervention on the earth was concerned. He was then limited to function as a Judge over the earth. This wasn't because God didn't have power and authority but because of His integrity. He had given authority to physical human beings, and to be true to His own Word, He did not take back His gift to mankind and say, "This is not the way I wanted it; time out, stop, we're going to do it all over." No, God bound Himself by His own Word. For, He upholds all things by the word of His power (Hebrews 1:3), the gifts and callings of God are without repentance. When He gives you a gift, He will not take is back even if you mess up. But He is always going to judge at the appointed time because He is a Righteous Judge and there is no partiality with Him.

THE SON OF MAN MANIFESTED

Throughout history God looked for someone He could flow through, but the problem was that all men were sinful and had yielded themselves to Satan. So, what was He to do? What God finally did was come to the earth Himself and become a man. This is tremendous when you understand it because now the devil was in big trouble. He had been using mankind's power, and God couldn't intervene directly to solve all these problems, because mankind was willfully and legally yielding his God-given authority to Satan. Satan was wrong in what he did, but people gave him the authority and power that was theirs.

But now, here came Jesus, and He was no longer only the Spirit but was in the form of physical flesh. This put the devil in a challenging situation because God not only had authority in heaven but becoming a Man gave Him authority on the earth. The Lord Jesus, in John 5:26-27, said:

"For as the Father hath life in himself; so hath he has given to the Son to have life in himself; And hath given him authority to execute judgment also, because he is the Son of man."

He was in this instant referring to His divinity and His physical body. Jesus came and exercised God-given authority. As the Son of Man, the Second Man, Jesus walked in absolute dominion and authority. When the devil came and looked, checking Jesus out to see if there was corruption in Him, the devil did not find any corruption in Jesus. He was from heaven.

MAN'S AUTHORITY REGAINED.

The devil tempted Jesus, and He never yielded to him. Satan lost in every battle with Him. Then at Calvary, Jesus took our sins on Himself, shed His blood and died to pay for them, went to hell snatched the keys of spiritual death from the hands of Satan and liberated the saint of old, rose again, and ascended to Heaven. Then He said in Matthew 28:18, *"All authority is given unto me in heaven and in the earth."* He won back for us the authority God had given mankind, which man lost to Satan, and as Savior of Mankind, Jesus now had all authority in heaven and on earth.

In the verse that follows Jesus' declaration of all authority in heaven and on earth belonging to Him, He said,

The Authority of the Believer

"Therefore, go and make disciples..." In effect, He was saying, "I now have all authority in heaven and earth, and I'm sharing it with you because you are in Me."

This time, however, there is a unique difference in the authority which God has given back to us as believers. It is a joint authority between us and the Lord Jesus Christ. It is no longer given to us solely as it was to Adam and Eve. They could give the authority away, allow the devil to oppress them, and basically be hopeless, but today our authority is shared with the Lord Jesus Christ. It is like having a joint bank account that requires both signatures in order to cash a check. Our authority is shared with the Lord Jesus, and His authority is shared with the church. Although we may fail, God is never again going to sign this authority over to the devil. For you who are in Christ, Satan has been rendered absolutely powerless. He has no ability to do anything in your life except what he deceives you in and what you voluntarily yield to. His number one weapon that he uses against your life is your ignorance about his defeat.

You need to recognize that you are the one who now has authority and power. Satan is fighting you with thoughts, and your weapons are such that you can take these thoughts captive. You can recognize that it is wrong for the devil to oppress you physically and find out what the Scripture has to say about healing or deliverance. John 8:32 says, *"And you shall know the truth, and the truth shall make you free."*

You're the one who has power and authority. God has given it to you, and I believe that the only thing that keeps you from exercising it is that you have not yet taken your thoughts captive. You have not used these spiritual truths to renew your mind and to realize what you have gotten. It is encouraging to find out that you are the one with authority and power. I pray that you will take this message, and meditate on it and that God will give you the revelation that you are the one that Satan trembles at. You should not be trembling at Satan, because you are the one who has the God-given power and authority on the earth. So, if you resist the devil, he will flee from you (James 4:7). Amen.

DOMINION EXERCISED

In my personal journey of seeking to understand and experience redemption, my life and ministry have been greatly impacted by the lives and ministries of other great men of God like Smith Wigglesworth and John G. Lake. These men of faith had a working revelation of their God-given authority and how to exercise it. So, here again, is another testimony from John G. Lake's book: *Adventures in God.*

"A woman came into the Healing Rooms once with a tumor larger than a full-grown unborn child. Her physicians had been fooled, believing it to be a child until nature's period had passed. Then they decided it must be something else. She came to the Healing Rooms and I interviewed her. She said, "Mr. Lake, I have the opinion of several physicians. They are all different, but each has said, 'It is possible it may be a child.' But now the time has passed, and they do not know what to say." I put my hand upon her for a moment, and I said, "Madame, it is not a child; it is a tumor." She sat down and wept. Her nurse was with her. Her soul was troubled, and she did not receive healing."

"She came back on another afternoon for prayer and returned the next day wearing her corsets. She said, "I came down to show you that I am perfectly normal. When I retired last night at 10 o'clock, there was no evidence that anything had taken place, beyond that I felt comfortable and the choking was gone. But when I awoke this morning, I was my normal size." I asked, "Did it disappear in the form of fluid?" She said, "There was not an outward sign of any character." Beloved, what happened to it? It dematerialized. The tumor dissolved. "

"What is a miracle? It is the tangible evidence of the supreme control of the Spirit of God over every character and form of materiality. Beloved, the power of such an event, such an act and sign, shows you and me that through living, positive, actual contact with the Spirit of God, all things are possible. Blessed be His Name!..."

The following testimony was a personal experience in the life of Smith Wigglesworth – the Apostle of Faith.

"One day he was suddenly struck with severe pain and was confined to his bed. Having agreed previously with his wife that no medications would be in his house, he left his healing in the hands of God."

"The family prayed all night for some relief, but none came. Smith grew weaker by the hour, and finally, he said to his wife, *"It seems to me that this is my home-call. To protect yourself, you should now call a physician."* Brokenhearted, Poly set out for a physician, believing the end had come for her husband."

"When the physician came, he shook his head and told the family that it was appendicitis and that the condition had been deteriorating for the past six months. He went on to say that Smith's organs were so damaged that there was no hope, not even with surgery. As the physician was leaving, an elderly woman and a young man came into Smith's room. This woman believed in praying the prayer of faith, and she believed that all sickness came from the devil. While she prayed, the young man got on the bed, laid both hands on Smith and cried, "Come out, devil, in the name of Jesus!"

"To Smith's great surprise, "the devil came out" and the pain was completely gone. For good measure, the couple prayed for Smith again, after which he got up, got dressed, and went downstairs. He said to his wife, "I am healed. Any work in?" as Poly heard his story, she, in total awe, handed him his job request. He then set out immediately to remedy the plumbing problem and was never again plagued with appendicitis." (God's Generals: Smith Wigglesworth – Apostle of Faith, by Roberts Lairdon).

Chapter 10

EXPERIENCING REDEMPTION

I thank my God, making mention of you always in my prayers, hearing of your love and faith which you have towards the Lord Jesus and towards all the saints, that the sharing [communication] of your faith may become effective by the acknowledgment of every good thing which is in you in Christ Jesus (Philemon 1:4-6)

In the pages of this book, I have attempted to communicate to you on the person of Jesus Christ and to show how, He, as our Redeemer has redeemed all those who are in Christ. In Chapter 2, I mentioned how I have come to see Him as God's *"ultimate Gift of love"* for the redemption of a hopelessly lost world that was under the sway of the devil and his associates. For, God demonstrated His love for us in that while we were yet in our sins, Christ died for us (Romans 5:8).

God's love for us is really much more than Jesus dying on the cross for the sins of the world. For, He came for the restoration of that which was lost. Jesus said, *"For the Son of man came to seek and to save what was lost."*

We have traditionally interpreted and applied these words of Jesus only to the salvation of perishing souls from the flames of hell. But He left His eternal glory, came to earth in a flesh and blood suit, demonstrated the love of the Father towards fallen humanity, took upon Himself all the sins, curses, sickness and diseases of the entire world; He was made sin for our sake, then went to the cross and died a criminals death so that we can be redeemed and that we may receive the power to become God's children. Here then, is where I believe is the premise for our invitation into experiencing redemption.

OUR RESPONSE IN LOVE THROUGH PRAISE

In Galatians 5:6, Apostle Paul teaches that faith works through love. So, when Paul heard of Philemon's love and the faith which he had towards Jesus and all the saints, he wrote him a letter in which he prayed for Philemon: that the communication of Philemon's faith may become effective by the acknowledging of every good thing which is in him

[Philemon] in Christ Jesus. Thus, I believe that a genuine love towards Jesus and all the saints is the springboard from which anyone may enter into an everyday experiential manifestation of redemption in Christ, if they continue steadfastly therein and in acknowledgment of every good thing that is in them in Christ Jesus.

You, who have been redeemed in Christ, also need to realize that your faith works through love: love towards Jesus and all the saints.

First, realize that faith works through the comprehension of how much love God has lavished on you, which is because of His great love with which He loved you (Ephesians 2:4). For, God so loved you that He gave His only begotten Son for your redemption (John 3:16), and *"He who did not spare His own Son, but delivered Him up for us all, how shall He not also with Him freely give us all things?"* (Romans 8:32). So, you need to be conscious of and be firmly grounded in the love of God towards you. Soak yourself in it and be immersed in God's unconditional love for you; "Because the love of God has been poured out in our hearts by the Holy Spirit who was given to us" (Romans 5:5). This reminds me of a quote from John G. Lake which says:

> "The life of the Christian without the indwelling power of the Spirit in the heart is a weariness to the flesh. It is

Experiencing Redemption

obedience to commandments and an endeavor to walk according to a pattern which you have no power to follow. But, bless God, the Christian life that is lived by the impulse of the Spirit of Christ within your soul, becomes a joy, a power, and a glory." (Adventures with God, by John G. Lake)

Secondly, you must respond to God's love in thanksgiving, praise and loving adoration for who Jesus is, and for how great His love has been poured out towards you, redeeming and reconciling you to God the Father. God's love, which has been poured out in your heart by the Holy Spirit must find expression through praise and worship. Spend quality time in building yourself up on your most holy faith through prayerful praise and worship; praying in the Holy Spirit; Who keeps you rooted and grounded in the love of God (Jude 1:20).

Thirdly, begin to acknowledge every good thing that is yours in Christ Jesus. These things are already in you, in your spirit-man (In the appendix section of this book, I have listed some of the good things which your redemption has made available in Christ). So, let your mind come into an agreement with the word of God concerning the realities of your redemption in Christ. This is because, the only way by which you may experience the realities of your redemption in Christ, the realities which have been deposited into your spirit-man, is through faith in the word of God. As you continue in prayerful worship and the acknowledgment of your redemption in Christ, you will sense a connection of your spirit-man with the Holy Spirit and a flow of the anointing of the Holy Spirit and with it a witness within your spirit-man of the realities of the finished work of Christ and your inheritance in Him. This is what is commonly called the glory realm; the realm of divinity; and the realm in which your oneness with Christ in the spirit is experienced. I believe this to be what Jesus meant when He *"Cried out, saying, 'If anyone thirsts, let him come to Me and drink. He who believes in Me, as the Scripture has said, out of his heart [spirit] will flow rivers of living water'"* (John 7:37-38).

It is in this realm, the realm of faith, that the communication of your faith may become effective in the release of virtue from the spiritual realm, to affect and influence the emotional and physical realms. It is in this realm that the miracle-working power of God is tapped into and released in the name of Jesus. It is also in this realm that the seven anointings of the Holy Spirit, which are enumerated for us in Isaiah 11:2, is tapped into: *"And the spirit of the Lord shall rest upon him, the spirit of wisdom and understanding, the spirit of counsel and might, the spirit of knowledge and of the fear of the Lord."*

Therefore, it is with these redemption realities in the spirit-man that the Bible goes to teach the following:

> "By faith, we understand that the worlds were framed by the word of God so that the things which are seen were not made of things which are visible" (Hebrews 11:3).
>
> "And whatever you ask in My name, that I will do, that the Father may be glorified in the Son. If you ask anything in My name, I will do it" (John 14:13, 14).
>
> "Whatever you ask the Father in My name He will give you. Until now you have asked nothing in My name. Ask, and you will receive, that your joy may be full." (John 16:23, 24)
>
> "And whatever things you ask in prayer, believing, you will receive" (Matthew 21:22).
>
> "Jesus said to him, if you can believe, all things are possible to him who believes" (Mark 9:23).
>
> "So, Jesus answered and said to them, "Have faith in God. For assuredly, I say to you, whoever says to this mountain, 'Be removed and be cast into the sea' and does not doubt in his heart but believes that those things he says will be done, he will have whatever he says. Therefore, I say to you, whatever things you ask when you pray, believe that you receive them, and you will have them" (Mark 11:22-24)

Experiencing Christ Jesus, The Redeemer

I have ministered to many people and seen God heal those who were in hopeless medical conditions. A lady, of whom I was informed was HIV positive was brought into a revival service in the town of Buea, Cameroon, where I was invited to speak as a guest speaker. She had been to many doctors and many other places for prayers. She was physically very weak and in great pain. I was told that she had not been to church for several months and the doctors had given up on her. After my preaching, I called for the sick to come up for prayers, and she was assisted to the front where a chair was brought for her to sit on. Together with the elders of the church in Buea, we laid our hands on her proclaiming over her the realities of her redemption in Christ and thanking God for the finished work of the cross.

I then took my authority in Christ and commanded the spirit of infirmity and HIV/AIDS to let her loose; I spoke to her body, commanding it to respond to the healing power of the Holy Spirit. After the ministration, no spectacular manifestation happened, except for the fact that she walked on her own to her seat even though she was still in pain. But after a few months, I was in another town, the town of Kumba, to accompany Professor Joseph Mbafor, who was ministering there. A young beautifully dressed and smiling lady came by to greet me. She introduced herself to me, but I could not make her out, then one of the elders with whom she came reminded me that she was the sister with the HIV case we prayed for. She was completely healed and healthy. She is HIV free, for, she had received her healing. Redemption has been experienced in her body. Hallelujah!

Another healing miracle I want to share with you was one that happened during a Bible study in my home in Riverdale, MD. A lady was invited by one of the sisters of the church to attend our Bible Studies. After the lesson of the evening, I asked for people to share their personal prayer needs so that we may join our faith with theirs in the prayer of agreement. This lady shared how she had an appointment to see a doctor the next day and she was afraid because of a lump on her left breast. I then asked my wife, Julienne, to feel the lump with her hand and to confirm, which she did. I further explained to the lady that God's power is the same for all sicknesses and diseases. It is the same power of God that heals a cold that will also heal cancer and tumors. It makes no difference to God. And I exhorted her to believe for her healing miracle to manifest.

My wife, Julienne, then placed her hand on the lump and repeated after me, declaring over her the realities of her redemption in Christ. She cursed the tumor and commanded it to disappear. With her hand still on the lump, she could feel the thing shrinking. Then, I asked the lady to feel the difference for herself, and her reaction was that she fell prostrate on the floor crying out for joy and praising God for His miracle and mercy. It is needless to say that she was healed. The next day, she went for her doctor's appointment and came back with a clean medical report. Praise the Lord!

APPENDIX A

YOU CAN RECEIVE CHRIST RIGHT NOW BY FAITH THROUGH PRAYER

If after reading this book and you have not received Jesus in your heart and life, I encourage you to do it right now. Accept Jesus as your Redeemer and make Him the Lord of your life. The very moment you do so, your spirit is reborn and brought into fellowship with the Father, the Almighty God. You become a Child of God. This will then put you in a position to receive from Him by faith all the promises that are in His Word.

Romans 10:9-10 says,

> That if thou shalt confess with thy mouth the Lord Jesus, and shalt believe in thine heart that God hath raised him from the dead, thou shalt be saved. For with the heart man

believeth unto righteousness; and with the mouth confession is made unto salvation (Romans 10:9-10 KJV).

Prayer is simply talking to God. God knows your heart and He is not as concerned with your words as He is with the attitude of your heart. So, talk to God in the sincerity of your heart. Confess your sins to Him, for He is faithful and just to forgive and cleanse you from all unrighteousness.

The following is a suggested prayer:

"Lord Jesus, I need You. I believe that you are the Son of God, that you died for my redemption and that you were raised from the dead. Thank You for dying on the cross for my sins. I repent of sin and I open the door of my life to receive You as my Savior and my Lord. Thank You for forgiving me and giving me eternal life. Take control of the throne of my life. Lord help me to become the kind of person You want me to be."

Does this prayer express the desire of your heart? If it does, I encourage you to be serious and pray this prayer right now and Christ will come into your life, as He has promised. Amen!

APPENDIX B

DECLARE WHO YOU ARE IN CHRIST?

The following biblical truths about your identity in Jesus Christ are derived from a few selected passages in the New Testament. I have included them here so that you may declare them over yourself in full assurance of faith. I encourage you to declare the "I Am Scriptures" and internalize them through prayer and meditation first, then, do the same with the "I Have Scriptures." If you can discipline yourself to do this, with conviction, over a 21-day period, I can guarantee you that your life will never be the same.

- I am a child of God. (John 1:12)
- I am born again in Christ (John 3:3)
- I am a branch of the true vine and a conduit of Christ's life. (John 15:1-5)
- I am a friend of Jesus Christ. (John 15:15)

- I am chosen, holy, and blameless before God. (Ephesians 1:4).
- I am redeemed and forgiven by the grace of our Lord Jesus Christ. (Ephesians 1:7)
- I am no longer under condemnation; I have been set free from the law of sin and death. (Romans 8:1-2)
- I am a joint heir with Christ. (Romans 8:17)
- I am joined to the Lord and am one spirit with Him. (1 Corinthians 6:17)
- I am a new creation in Christ. (2 Corinthians 5:17)
- I am no longer a slave but a child and an heir of God. (Galatians 4:7)
- I am seated in the heavenly places with Christ, far above principalities and powers. (Ephesians 2:6; 2:21)
- I am God's workmanship created in Christ to produce good works. (Ephesians 2:10)
- I am a member of Christ's body and a partaker of His promises. (Ephesians 3:6; Ephesians 5:30)
- I am a citizen of heaven in Christ. (Philippians 3:20)
- I am the righteousness of God in Christ. (2 Corinthians 5:21).
- I am a minister of reconciliation in Christ (2 Corinthians 5:19).
- I am an ambassador for Christ (2 Corinthians 5:20).

- I am an heir to the promises of God in Christ (Romans 4:13).
- I am a co-worker with God in the proclamation and the demonstration of the Kingdom of God on earth. (1 Corinthians 3:9; 2 Corinthians 6:1)
- I am a beneficiary of the New Covenant which was ratified in the blood of Jesus Christ for my redemption, sanctification, and adoption into God's glorious family (Hebrews 2:10).
- I am more than a conqueror in Christ Jesus. For greater is He who is in me than he who is in the world (Romans 8:37; 1 John 4:4).
- I am an overcomer in Christ Jesus my Lord in who I share in all His victories (1 John 4:4).

- I have been justified and redeemed in Christ. (Romans 3:23-24; Romans 6:6).
- I have been accepted by Christ. (Romans 15:7).
- I have been called, sanctified by God the Father, and preserved in Jesus Christ (Jude 1:1)
- I have received an abundance of grace and the gift of righteousness in Christ by which I reign in life with Christ (Romans 5:17).

- I have been called to be a saint in Christ (1 Corinthians 1:2; Ephesians 1:1; Philippians 1:1; Colossians 1:2)
- I have wisdom, righteousness, sanctification, and redemption in Christ. (1 Corinthians 1:30)
- I have become the righteousness of God in Christ. (2 Corinthians 5:21)
- I have been made one with all who are in Christ Jesus. (Galatians 3:28)
- I have been set free in Christ. (Galatians 5:1)
- I have been blessed with every spiritual blessing in the heavenly places in Christ. (Ephesians 1:3)
- I have been predestined by God to obtain an inheritance in Christ. (Ephesians 1:9-11)
- I have been sealed with the Holy Spirit of promise in Christ. (Ephesians 1:13)
- I have been made alive with Christ. (Ephesians 2:4-5)
- I have boldness and confident access into God's presence through faith in Christ. (Ephesians 3:12)
- I have been brought near to God by the blood of Christ. (Ephesians 2:13)
- I have been made complete in Christ. (Colossians 2:9-10)

- I have been washed, sanctified, and justified in the name of the Lord Jesus and by the Spirit of our God (1 Corinthians 6:11)
- I have been perfected forever in Christ (Hebrews 10:14)
- I have been redeemed from the Law of Sin and Death (Romans 8:2).
- I have been redeemed from the oppressive power of all sicknesses and diseases. (Hebrews 9:12; 1 Peter 2:24)
- I have been redeemed from all curses operating in my family bloodline and from every curse on the earth. (Galatians 3:13; Hebrews 9:12)
- I have been redeemed from all the powers of darkness (Colossians 1:13).
- I have been redeemed from the domain of the powers of the prince of the air (Colossians 1:13).
- I have been raised up from the dead and seated with Christ in heavenly places. (Colossians 3:1)
- I have been chosen by God, and I am holy and beloved. (Colossians 3:12).
- I have been given authority to use the name of Jesus for the glory of God the Father (Philippians 2:10-11).
- I have been given power and authority against all unclean spirits (Matthew 10:1).

- I have been given authority in Christ to heal the sick, raise the dead and cleanse the lepers (Matthew 10:1; Mark 16:18).
- I have been given authority in Christ to overcome all the powers of the devil and his kingdom (Luke 10:19).

ABOUT THE AUTHOR

Pastor James Ekor-Tah is a gifted and dynamic Bible teacher who is deeply burdened for the believers, especially those he pastors, to know the truth about God's word, so that they may live a victorious life in Christ. His passion is to see the lost saved, the sick healed, the distressed relieved, the broken restored, the oppressed delivered and the discouraged empowered to victory.

His vision is to see whole families come to Christ and serve him with all their hearts. Above all, as a missionary, he is committed to the worldwide vision of the Christian Missionary Fellowship International (CMFI), to make disciples of all nations. Consequently, he works hard to establish a solid multi-ethnic congregation with the same missionary vision.

Pastor James is married to his sweet-heart Julienne Abigail who is a dynamic woman of God and a faithful partner

About the Author

in the ministry which God has entrusted unto them. They are blessed parents of three beautiful girls; Elizabeth Grace and Madeleine Shekinah, Jamie Rhema.